A Guide to ....ing
A HAPPY, WELL-TRAINED DOG

PUP PARENTING

LYNN LOTT and JANE NELSEN,
authors of the best-selling "Positive Discipline" parenting series,

AND ANIMAL BEHAVIORIST THERRY JAY

RODALE

© 2006 by Lynn Lott, Jane Nelsen, and Therry Jay

Cover photograph © American Images Inc./Getty Images

Book design by Drew Frantzen

Library of Congress Cataloging-in-Publication Data
    Lott, Lynn.
        Pup parenting : a guide to raising a happy, well-trained dog / Lynn Lott and Jane Nelsen, and Therry Jay.
            p.   cm.
        Includes index.
        ISBN-13 978-1-59486-081-2 paperback
        ISBN-10 1-59486-081-5 paperback
        1. Puppies. 2. Puppies—Training.   I. Nelsen, Jane.   II. Jay, Therry.   III. Title.
        SF427.L674   2006
        636.7'07—dc22   2005031210

Distributed to the trade by Holtzbrinck Publishers

2   4   6   8   10   9   7   5   3   1   paperback

We inspire and enable people to improve their lives and the world around them
For more of our products visit **rodalestore.com** or call 800-848-4735

To Buddy, Magic, My Son, and Britt,
the dogs who changed our lives

CONTENTS

ACKNOWLEDGMENTS

People often wonder how a book takes form. This book was written in three stages: the beginning, the middle, and the end. In the beginning, Lynn Lott spent hours asking Therry Jay questions about parenting dogs, and Therry kindly and patiently answered all of them while Lynn typed every word as furiously as she could. This went on for several years. Lynn put together proposal after proposal, but the book didn't find a home, so the two women sadly put the book to rest.

In the middle, Lynn tried to revise the book, combining doggy discipline with parenting tips. Once again, the book didn't find a home. Then, with the help of Trish (T. J.) MacGregor and the stars, Lynn discovered June Clark, who not only became her agent, but made publishing this book possible. June had recently become a doggy parent herself, and she was relentless in helping Lynn put together a proposal that could sell. With her assistance, the book found a home at Rodale.

The end of the writing process was the most fun. It took almost two years. By then, Therry had moved on to work with horses, so Lynn started the search for another writing partner. She didn't have to look far. She and Jane Nelsen had written four other parenting books together, and both have taught parenting for over thirty years. They are a formidable team. It took some arm-twisting to get Jane on board, but in the end, she consented, and made the homestretch more fun and exciting than Lynn imagined possible.

The information in this book is based on the authors' personal experiences and stories from real people about real dogs, although names and breeds have been changed on some occasions at the pup parents' request. We are grateful for all those parents who so willingly contributed to our effort. We'd also like to thank Dr. Russ Gurevitch, Dr. Mary Press, Dr. Barbara Farrel, and the staff at Larkspur Landing Veterinary Clinic for their expertise and help. Thanks to June Clark for finding a home for our book, Joan Woodard for her two-day writing– and research–support marathon in the homestretch, and our editor, Jennifer Kushnier, who demanded excellence and stuck with us till she got it. Jennifer, we're better writers for your guidance and persistence.

Lynn couldn't enjoy being a dog mommy (or writer) as much as she does without the partnership and endless help from her husband, Hal Penny. She is also grateful to the Adlerian and Dreikursian psychologists and parent educators who took punishment out of parenting and coupled firmness and kindness to empower young people. Their methods work well with dogs, too.

Lynn enjoyed surfing the Web, finding one exciting site after another with support for pup parents. (How times have changed since her first dog, Beau Spot, almost forty years ago!) She chuckled her way through the books of dog quotes and enjoyed brushing up on current obedience-training methods in both *The Only Dog Training Book You'll Ever Need* by Gerilyn J. Bielakiewicz and *The Guide to Beginning Obedience* by Nikki Moustaki. [Sorry, Gerilyn, but I used two training books! —L.L.]

Lynn, an avid mystery reader, finds irresistible those authors who love dogs and put them in their books. Thanks to Robert Parker and Carl Hiaasen who not only understand dogs, but the people who parent them. Finally, a special thanks to Richard Russo for his hysterical prologue in *Straight Man: A Novel*. It's a must-read for anyone who has children who have ever begged for a dog.

Therry's heroes in the dog-training world are Jean Donaldson (Therry wants everyone to read her book, *Culture Clash*, from cover to cover, at least six times), Karen Pryor, Sue Sternberg, William Campbell, Ian Dunbar, Patricia B. McConnell, and Terry Ryan. When Therry left training dogs behind to work with horses, pooch parents lost a great resource. Fortunately, her thoughts are collected in this book, and really, she's only a phone call away.

Although Jane joined this project with reservations (a dog hasn't been part of her family since all the kids left home), she couldn't help but get caught up in Lynn's enthusiasm for how the positive parenting skills work with canine kids as well as the two-legged kind. Jane really saw the picture when she heard so many stories about "the boys"—two black Labs in the family of her daughter and son-in-law, Mary and Mark Tamborski. She'd also like to thank her son Ken for recounting his story about his night in the canyon, and her son Brad for sharing his experiences with the family dalmatian.

We hope you'll enjoy reading this book as much as we enjoyed writing it.

Lynn, Therry, and Jane

INTRODUCTION

MAKE THE MOVE FROM PACK LEADER TO PUP PARENT

"They're nice to have—a Dog."

—*F. Scott Fitzgerald*, The Great Gatsby

Hello, pup parents!

You know who you are. We run into you daily.

We hear you talking about your "boys," "the baby," "the kids," "my little punkin'," and as we listen more closely, we find that you are referring to your dogs, not your human children. Sometimes, you explain that your dog is like the child you never had or a better companion than the husband you used to have.

We see you walking at the park, your dog on a leash, glued to your side, attentive and wanting to please you. Your dog remains calm when people or other dogs approach, and when she stops to relieve herself, we see you picking up after her. You talk to your dog in a quiet, encouraging voice, and she wags her tail in confirmation.

We see you in the airports, with your dog in a little carrier, dressed in his travel shirt, ready to vacation with you. Everyone fusses over your dog while they wait for their baggage, and you have the face of the proudest mommy or daddy on earth.

We find you at the pet store, loaded down with toys, pillows, harnesses, treats, and bags of food. Often your dog is with you, keeping you company while you shop.

We see you in the outdoors and on the trails. You have a pack on your back, and your dog has saddlebags. Your dog stays on the trail and doesn't run off to disturb the wildlife. We see you on the rivers and lakes, with your dog in your boat, looking for all the world like the most contented being in the universe.

We see your dogs in your car or truck, safely ensconced in a harness, behind a doggy gate, or attached to a bolt in your truck bed. Sometimes your dog waits in the car for you, weather permitting. We notice the windows are slightly open and your dog has a large dish of water next to him. He's usually sitting in the driver's seat, waiting patiently for your return.

If this describes your dog or your relationship with her, like we said, *Hello, pup parents*. That's you! If your dog doesn't behave like the ones we have described so far, don't despair. If it's what you want, you *can* have it, but it will take some effort and, quite possibly, a change in your attitude, too.

Many doggy parents aren't interested in the old methods of being a pack leader—acting like an alpha dog, asserting dominance in the pack. Doggy parents don't see themselves as one of the dogs, nor do they feel a need to be top dog. They are a leader in the family, using their human intelligence and compassion to parent their pups. They are not comfortable using abusive methods to train their dogs.

On the other hand, some are afraid their dogs will be wild and undisciplined if they don't use the punitive methods recommended by many "experts." Because of this dilemma, they end up being a lot like human parents, vacillating from one extreme to the other, mired in guilt and exasperation. You don't have to go this route. There is another option: kind and firm pup parenting.

How is kind and firm pup parenting different from other methods of training your dog? Other methods refer to your dog as a pet or an "it." They refer to you as a pet owner or a pack leader. In *Pup Parenting*, we describe a very different relationship with dogs. You are no longer a pet owner or one of the doggy gang. You are now a doggy parent. Your dog is a member of your family, not a pet or an object!

Being a pup parent involves new responsibilities. You need to treat your dog with respect. You need to stop reacting to problems and instead, plan ahead for difficulties that might arise. You'll have to stop looking for blame and start working on solutions. You may even need to give up some of the more traditional methods you used in the past or watched your parents use when they brought a dog into your family.

Relationship changes start with you, not your dog. This is the core of *Pup Parenting*. We're sure you'd like to be the best doggy parent you can be and that you want to have a well-behaved dog. But it will take some work on your part. Whatever you practice, you'll get better at, but if you're lazy and don't practice anything, that's exactly what you'll excel at—nothing.

Bottom line: Your dog changes as you change! There's that saying that you can't teach an old dog new tricks, but we know you can teach your dog, old or young, just about anything when you learn new tricks to *change yourself first*. By making small changes, step-by-step, with the aid of this book, you'll experience major successes with your canine kids, and we're here to help you do that.

Together and separately, for more than thirty years, we've been helping people improve their relationships with their children, whether they are canine or human. We teach methods based on kindness and firmness, nonpunitive follow-through, an understanding of the needs of dogs to belong and be special in the family without running over the family, and the notion that the parent sets the culture for the family instead of reacting to the dog.

We can't promise you will have a perfect dog (after all, dogs will be dogs) anymore than we could promise that parents will have perfect children (kids will be kids). We can promise, however, that you will develop unique "parenting skills" that will help you solve doggy dilemmas and improve your dog's behavior. Overall, you will have a happier relationship with your dog!

Pup Parenting is the first parenting book written for doggy moms and dads. It's a dog book with heart. Whether you have a new puppy or an old bloodhound lying at your feet, you'll find something that enhances your effectiveness as a parent and brightens your day.

CHAPTER 1

WHAT'S *YOUR* PUP PARENTING STYLE?

"With proper training, man can become dog's best friend."

—Etched onto a plaque on a popular dog-walking trail in Jupiter Beach, Florida

It all starts with you: Parents set the culture in which a dog grows and develops. Some people think we're barking up the wrong tree when we keep pointing out that change begins with you. However, from years of experience, we know you'll be amazed how quickly your dog changes when *you* behave differently.

How you parent your dog has a huge influence on how the dog behaves. If you don't like the direction things are going with your dog, here's the big news: First you'll have to change yourself. Like the opening quote says, with proper training, you can become your dog's best friend.

First, you need to be clear on what kind of pup parent you are. The little test on pages 2–3 will help you discover your strengths and areas of weakness when parenting your canine. Your score tells you whether your dog may be training you or if you are on your way to the kind of training that meets your dog's needs along with

(continued on page 4)

Read each question carefully and then answer with Always, Sometimes, or Never.

1. I have a well-thought-out philosophy about dog rearing.

   Always   Sometimes   Never

2. I use nonpunitive discipline to train my dog.

   Always   Sometimes   Never

3. I am kind and firm when teaching behaviors to my dog.

   Always   Sometimes   Never

4. If someone listened to me talking to my dog, they would hear a calm voice instead of a raised voice, begging, pleading, or whining.

   Always   Sometimes   Never

5. I am consistent when I teach my dog.

   Always   Sometimes   Never

6. I make sure my dog gets daily exercise.

   Always   Sometimes   Never

7. I understand that my dog needs more than just love.

   Always   Sometimes   Never

8. I consistently use my training cues.

   Always   Sometimes   Never

9. I keep my temper in check.

   Always   Sometimes   Never

10. I give a cue only when I'm prepared to enforce it immediately.

    Always   Sometimes   Never

11. I expect a response on the first cue.

Always   Sometimes   Never

12. When walking my dog, I keep a loose leash.

Always   Sometimes   Never

13. My dog doesn't pull on the leash.

Always   Sometimes   Never

14. I avoid calling my dog for the purpose of scolding or reprimanding him in any way.

Always   Sometimes   Never

15. I avoid overstimulating my dog.

Always   Sometimes   Never

Evaluating your score:

If you answered Always to most of the questions, you are a proactive dog parent who is already using effective, nonpunitive discipline and, still, you are open to learning even more.

If Sometimes was your favorite answer, pat yourself on the back. You've got a lot going for you and will find the information in this book helpful and easy to apply.

A combination of Always, Sometimes, and Never shows that you really want to be a good dog parent, but you need more knowledge and skills until respectful methods seem as comfortable to you as an old shoe. To acquire the skills you want, you'll need to set a time for you and your dog to work a little each day to make changes. Practice, practice, practice to be the best pooch parent you can be.

If you answered Never to most questions, first, give your dog a ribbon for training you. Then get serious. Your dog is running the house. Is that really okay with you? And is it really good for your dog?

your own. The test is quick and easy to take (and there are no failing grades, either).

The test helps you zero in on how you think about your dog. What does your dog mean to you? For some of you, your dog is your best friend, one of your kids, a family member. Others of you might think of your dog as just another farm animal that lives outdoors. Maybe your dog has never seen the outdoors except to relieve herself (or maybe not even then if you've paper-trained her). Whether your dog is part of the family or living outdoors, how you think about her has a huge impact on your relationship with her and on your parenting style. If you are like many pup parents, led by your emotions—loving and cuddling one second, and yelling in frustration the next—you're going to have some work to do. You'll have to start considering what is best for your dog not only in the moment, but also in the long-term.

Pinpoint Your Parenting Style

Have you ever wondered if you are doing a good job with your dog? Our guess is that your answer is yes. Why else would you be attracted to a book on parenting your canine kid? Parenting is the most important job in the world, yet it involves the least amount of education. Savvy parents know it is important to learn as much about parenting as possible. Your education begins by looking at your current parenting style and making sure it's the one you prefer. Yes, parents of canine kids have a parenting style, just as parents of human kids do.

If someone were to ask you to describe your parenting style, how would you answer? We'll focus on three different styles and help you pinpoint yours. We won't discuss neglectful parenting, because we know if that were your style, you wouldn't be reading this book. Once you discover your style, you can decide if it is right for you and your pup. Review the options and consider whether you'd like to change your style. When you understand the differences, you can move from one style to another.

Which of the following three parenting types best describes you?

1. **Top Dog:** You see yourself as the center of the universe with all the power.

2. **Milquetoast:** Your dog is the center of the universe with all the power.

3. **Kind and Firm:** Your dog is part of your family, not the center of the universe. You know your dog's personality and create boundaries without breaking your dog's spirit.

If you haven't identified your style yet, the following exaggerated caricatures may help you figure out whether your style is Top Dog, Milquetoast, or Kind and Firm.

Top Dog Dave is clearly the center of the universe and has all the power. His dog lives outside and spends hours alone in his dog run. When his dog whimpers, barks, or jumps on Dave, he grabs him by the scruff of his neck, shakes him, throws him to the ground, and shows him who is top dog. Dave keeps his dog run clean, makes sure his dog has fresh water and food each day, and spends time with him when it's convenient for Dave. Dave's dog isn't considered part of the family. He's a dog, an object, livestock. Is your style like Top Dog Dave's?

Milquetoast Myra's dog runs the family. Her dog has only to whimper softly and Myra picks her up and carries her from room to room. She (mind you, we're referring to the dog here) has her own trainer, masseuse, monogrammed pillow and bowl, and won't leave Myra alone for a minute. Myra's dog calls all the shots. Does this sound like you?

Kind and Firm Kathy's dog is part of the family but not the center of the universe. Kathy spent time obedience training her dog. She takes the dog to the dog park each day and walks him three times a day. He goes to doggy day care when she works extra long hours, but he also spends time home alone sleeping on his pillow and playing with his toys. Kathy and her dog are welcome everywhere. The dog can be playful or quiet, depending on the needs of the situation. Is this your parenting style?

The methods in this book reflect Kind and Firm Kathy's approach. There is, however, room for a lot of variation. Each style, even Kathy's, has strengths along with areas that could use improvement. Perfection is an illusion. Learning and growing with your pup is what it's all about. We believe you can be a great pup parent regardless of your parenting style as long as you practice kindness and firmness at the same time. Kindness shows respect for your dog, and firmness shows respect for you, for others, and for the needs of the situation. That's what *Pup Parenting* is all about.

Is It Time to Make Some Changes?

By now you may have discovered that you'd like to make some changes. Even with desire, change still takes time and work. One of the most difficult concepts for pup parents is that any lasting change requires time for training. This means practice, practice, practice until you and your pooch are used to doing things differently. Even though you may be tempted to try to change more than one habit at a time, we recommend picking one to work on and giving it your full attention. Although it seems like a lot of work, and it is in the beginning, the results are well worth the effort in the long run.

Some pup parents want to make changes, but they procrastinate until something scary happens that shocks them into behaving differently. We call this a moment of truth. Any crisis can be an opportunity to learn and grow. Is that how it is for you? Do you need a crisis to get your attention, as did Bliss, mother of a seven-month-old toy poodle named Peaches? One day Bliss and her daughter Melanie were playing in the front yard when they noticed that Peaches was nowhere to be seen. After looking everywhere, they spotted the little poodle down the street about to run in front of a stream of traffic. Bliss screamed, "Peaches, come here," a command that was ignored by the little dog, off on her own adventures. Peaches darted across the street and then back again, cars swerving to avoid her and brakes squealing. When lucky little Peaches was finally firmly in her mommy's arms, Bliss realized she had been given another chance with her little dog.

Bliss began hanging a leash on a hook by the front door to help her remember to use it each time she went outside with Peaches. Then she called her friends to get the name of a good puppy training program and signed the two of them up for the next session. She told her kids that once she and Peaches started their class, they would have to practice walking with the leash every day. She asked that her kids let her work with Peaches until the pup was trained. She promised she would then help her children learn how to use the leash properly so they could take Peaches for walks, too. Finally, she asked her husband to fence in a small area in the backyard where Peaches and the kids could safely play without the fear of traffic accidents. Her moment of truth helped her realize she had to be much more proactive to keep Peaches safe.

We know dogs can't really talk, but sometimes we like to imagine what they might say if they could.

If Peaches could talk, what would she say? "Whew! That was a close call, but, it was exciting, too. I don't think I could resist doing that again without some help from my family."

Some Changes Take Time

Not everyone needs a crisis to make changes. Some pup parents are like Hank, who made up his mind to stay a step ahead of his dog once he realized his one-year-old Akita, Otis, was getting the best of him by escaping from his dog yard while Hank was at work. It wasn't easy. If you have a dog as clever as Otis, you know just what we're talking about.

Hank had always thought of himself as a mild-mannered guy, but Otis was such an accomplished escape artist that his antics were bringing out another side of Hank that he didn't like at all. At first, each time Otis ran away, Hank continued his family's dog training tradition and rolled up his own newspaper and swatted Otis harshly, shouting, "No, no! Bad dog!" To his dismay, the newspaper had no noticeable effect on the Akita. Even more surprising, Hank discovered that he didn't feel good about hitting his dog. He started reading more about training dogs and decided to give positive, nonpunitive methods a try, even though he knew it would require major work on his part.

Like many parents, Hank got a lot of chances to practice his own behavioral changes, as Otis kept finding new ways to get out of his enclosed area. Hank had heard that change is what keeps you young, so he had a lot to appreciate since Otis continued to provide him with opportunities to drink from the fountain of youth.

THE WRONG (SHORT-TERM) QUESTIONS THAT KEEP YOU STUCK

1. How do I *make* my dog "mind"?

2. How do I *make* my dog understand "no"?

3. How do I *make* my dog listen to me?

4. How do I *get my dog to* cooperate (do what I say)?

5. How do I *make* this problem go away?

6. What is the *punishment*/consequence for this situation?

After reading the questions, you might ask, "What's wrong with them? They seem perfectly legitimate to me." What's wrong with them is that you can't move on to proactive, savvy parenting until you ask yourself the right questions in the box opposite. Notice the difference in the parenting approach, when you consider those questions.

THE RIGHT QUESTIONS THAT LEAD TO SAVVY PARENTING

1. How do I use this problem as an opportunity for learning for both me and my dog so we can see mistakes as opportunities to try again?

2. What is a way to help my dog fit into our family without using violent behaviors?

3. How can I respect myself and still respect my dog and his needs?

4. What resources are available to me that emphasize kindness and firmness for dog training?

But it was hard for Hank to make the necessary changes (as it would be for you), because he asked himself the wrong questions, like those in the box opposite. Thinking that way kept him in a reactive leadership role, rather than in a kind and firm pup parenting role.

When Hank began asking himself the "right" questions, he started seeing possibilities. Educated pup parents, like educated human parents, must learn how to stay a step ahead of their charges so that they can be better parents. Hank used his carpentry skills to build a special enclosure for Otis that would provide sun, shade, and plenty of room to stretch and play.

But just because Hank changed his behavior from a punitive reaction to positive prevention didn't mean that Otis was going to behave differently right away. He was used to doing things his way, and he escalated the game when Hank took charge. It's not unusual for things to get worse before they get better, and that's exactly what happened.

Otis figured out how to escape by digging a large hole under the fence. When Hank came home from work and saw Otis stretched out peacefully on the front porch, his first response was to grab the newspaper lying on the step next to the dog and revert to his old methods. Then Hank remembered that he had decided to be proactive instead of abusive, and to keep at it until he succeeded.

It also helped to remember something he read in one of the dog training books: Otis's behavior wasn't personal, and he wasn't trying to make a fool out of Hank. It was a breed thing. Akitas hate being cooped up.

Hank figured out how he could modify the enclosure. He fixed the hole and added another board for extra height, but the next day, Otis jumped over the fence. Hank added a latch to the gate, but Otis figured out how to reach up and undo it. At first Hank thought someone might be letting Otis out, but he peeked around the corner and spotted Otis on his hind legs, reaching over and unhooking the gate with his paw. Instead of wanting to hit Otis this time, Hank laughed out loud, celebrating his dog's ingenuity.

Finally, Hank knew how to get a step ahead of Otis. He put a stick in the latch so Otis couldn't open the gate. He was sure Otis would stay in his yard this time, but when Hank came home from work, he discovered Otis had figured out how to stand on a planter and climb over the taller fence. Hank shook his head, moved the planter, and added another board to make the fence even higher, for good measure. That was the magic touch. This time Otis stayed put. Even though Hank was persistent and clever, change took time to get a step ahead of Otis.

If Otis could talk, what might he say? "I'm sure glad my dad isn't a macho dude who exchanges his newspaper for something worse, like a chain. Getting into a pissing contest with a dog like me could be a real disaster."

Some Change Needs Assistance

Not everyone is willing to put in the time Hank did to make changes. Nor is everyone able to help their doggy learn new behaviors even when they do put in the time. Sometimes change requires outside assistance, and there's plenty of that around. You can hire an in-home trainer or behavior consultant. You can sign up for obedience-training classes. You can even send your dog away to be trained by an expert at doggy boarding school like Mallory did.

Mallory's toy poodle, Trixie, was so willful that when Mallory tried to get her to do what she wanted, Trixie curled her lip and snarled. Although it was hard not to laugh at a three-pound dog acting so ferociously, Mallory knew that Trixie was going to be a dog no one wanted to be around if she didn't nip this behavior in the bud. When Trixie chomped down hard enough to break the skin of Mallory's Bouvier des Flandres, Stevie, Mallory had to face facts. Trixie needed a different kind of help than Mallory could provide. She sent Trixie to a board-and-train school. By the time she returned home to Mallory, Trixie could hold a down stay (see page 137) with any kind of distraction, including kids on bikes, cats, and tempting food bribes. Her trainer worked with Mallory and Trixie on three separate occasions to help Mallory learn how to maintain the training.

Mallory said that the money spent on the school was the best investment she could have made. Not only was Trixie noticeably different after three weeks away, but Mallory was highly motivated to protect her investment by maintaining the changes she knew the little dog had worked so hard to achieve.

Making Changes Requires a Realistic Attitude

A true pup parent forms a relationship with the dog and is flexible, open, curious, and nondefensive. Examine your fantasies that you have or had when you first got your dog. Do any of these sound familiar?

"My dog will protect me."

"My dog will follow me everywhere."

"My dog will be my best friend."

"My dog will depend on me."

"My dog will play with me."

"My dog will live outside."

"My dog will stay off the furniture."

"My dog will never beg."

"My dog will never jump up on people."

Perhaps your dog magically did all the things you expected without any effort, but we doubt it. All the doggy parents we talked to have a story about a surprise (or two or ten) that came with their dogs. Here are some of our favorites: finding out that the dog's preferred food was inside the baby's diaper; discovering that the dog ate the cushions to their favorite chair while they were at work; noticing that the dog took toys away from other dogs at the dog park, making both parent and canine kid extremely unpopular; realizing that every time they wanted some privacy with their sweetie, the dog jumped up on the bed and snuggled in between them. In hindsight, it all seems funny, but at the time, some of the escapades were enough to make any pup parent tear out his or her hair—or worse yet, think about giving the dog away.

Do your fantasies match your current reality? If not, it's time to face reality and give up the daydream. Take your lead from the dog, acknowledging and enjoying the uniqueness of each creature. Don't be afraid to admit change might be needed. Tell yourself that change is fun, exciting, an opportunity to meet a challenge and grow, a way to feel alive, and worth the effort. Remind yourself that change is part of life, always possible, and that it's never too late to change.

Kind and Firm Pup Parenting in Action

Take a minute and review the questions in the test on page 9. Each question describes a kind and firm pup parent. Kind and firm pup parents are proactive, respectful, nonpunitive, and action-oriented. In the next chapter, we'll go into detail about how to achieve these four qualities. For now, consider them a concept, something you are striving for. As you read the following example of how a mom became a kind and firm pup parent, see if you can identify how she was proactive, respectful, nonpunitive, and action-oriented.

Amber, mother of three, attended parenting classes when her youngest was a toddler. She learned and practiced proactive, kind, and firm parenting with her children. She would never think they were cute if they were destroying someone else's property. Yet when she became a pooch parent to an adorable Labrador/spaniel mix puppy, she forgot about her Kind and Firm Kathy parenting style and acted more like Milquetoast Myra. (Remember her?) Amber wasn't even aware of how permissive she had become with her doggy kid.

She expected everyone to put up with her puppy's misbehavior, including what she called his "little mistakes." She named her pup Trouble because he couldn't seem to stop getting into it. Watching his antics gave her hours of pleasure, which she was sure everyone would enjoy as as much she did. When her friend Julie discovered a couple of Trouble's "little mistakes" on her bedroom carpet, and told Amber she couldn't visit anymore if she brought her dog along, Amber realized she was now the one in trouble. She had to do something about her puppy so she wouldn't hurt her friendship.

The most obvious solution would have been for Amber to leave Trouble at home when she visited her friend, but like many new parents, she wasn't ready for that. She felt protective of the little puppy and wanted to show off her new baby to her friend, whom she was sure would fall in love with him once he behaved better. She needed a plan, but she wasn't sure what to do next. Have you ever been in that same spot, where it's obvious that change is needed but you're not sure what to do?

When that happens, here's what we suggest. Take a step back and clarify what the problem is. It's close to impossible to make changes while you're in the middle of a mess. If you stop what you are doing, take a breath, and become an observer of your own situation, often solutions will jump right out at you. That's the definition of being proactive, which is what Amber was. When she took a step back and clarified the problems she was having with Trouble, she realized her problem was multi-layered. Trouble was making mistakes in the house and needed to complete his potty training. Amber was straining her relationship with her friend, a not-uncommon pup parenting issue. Amber was also suffering from her fear of letting go and leaving her baby at home. What parent hasn't encountered at least one of these problems, if not all of them?

When Amber stepped back, her nonpunitive options became clearer. She knew that with continued practice at her own house, her puppy would learn that going potty was something that needed to be done outside. She was also clear that eventually she'd be ready to leave her dog home with the kids or a doggy sitter. She remembered being just as skittish with all of her children when they were babies, but once they got a little older, she had no problem leaving them with a sitter. What she needed to focus on now was how to be more respectful of her friend's needs when she brought her dog to visit. She decided to ask Julie if she could bring a playpen over for Trouble to stay in while the two visited.

Julie was leery, and rightly so, as she had to have professional carpet cleaners in on both occasions that Amber and Trouble had visited, and that wasn't okay with her. But Amber was persistent, and eventually Julie agreed to try again. Amber showed she was now action-oriented by bringing a playpen and a large plastic drop cloth to put underneath it to Julie's house. Within a month, Trouble was out of the playpen, accident free, and the carpets remained pristine. And Amber and Julie are still friends.

Right about now you may be thinking that the solution either required too much effort or that it was too simplistic. But we know that as a pooch parent, you are willing to do the work it takes to raise your dog to be a good companion and a good guest. In the next chapter, we'll introduce you to our Five-Step Pup Parenting Plan that will help you find new parenting options just like Amber did (and like Bliss did on page 7).

If Trouble could talk, he might say: "I like the playpen. It's for babies, and that's what I am. It makes me feel secure."

In the next chapter, we'll explore the four common mistakes that pup parents make and show you how to correct them by using the Five-Step Pup Parenting Plan. As you become comfortable with the five-step plan, you'll soon be on the road to success. For now, if you haven't already, take the little test at the beginning of the chapter, give your pup parenting style a name, and decide what you want to work on. It's not important that you be a perfect parent. Great parenting has always been a step-by-step process. Your job is to work on the small steps that will move you in the direction of being a kind and firm pup parent.

KIND AND FIRM PUP PARENTING PRINCIPLES

1. It's always better for you to be training your dog instead of your dog training you.

2. Your attitude about your dog is reflected in your parenting style and the kind of relationship you have with your pup.

3. Kind and firm pup parenting requires being proactive, respectful, nonpunitive, and action-oriented.

4. To change a problem situation, start by taking a step back.

5. Replace striving for perfection with taking small steps as the way to change your relationship with your dog.

CHAPTER 2

THE FOUR MISTAKES PUP PARENTS MAKE AND A PLAN TO CORRECT THEM

"Hello. My name is No, No Bad Dog. What's yours?"

—*Anonymous*

"What happened to my fantasy dog—the one who loves me madly, but never misbehaves?" Your dog might ask another question: "What happened to my fantasy parent who knows all about dogs and wants to help me be a good companion?" And your cute little new puppy wonders: "When is someone going to show me how to get along in this family instead of yelling at me all the time and hitting me with that rolled-up newspaper?" When everyone wonders what happened, it is possible that you are suffering from one or all of the four common mistakes that parents make: being reactive instead of proactive, being disrespectful, being punitive, and talking instead of acting.

If you are making these mistakes, you can easily learn to correct them and improve your pup parenting by using our Pup Parenting Plan. With it, you'll learn lots of new tricks. By making a small change with the help of the steps, you'll experience major successes with your canine kids.

When you use the Pup Parenting Plan, you'll already be ahead because you will *start* by having a plan instead of trying to crisis-manage your pooch. You'll soon realize that your dog doesn't need to suffer to learn, because the solutions you'll use won't be abusive or punitive, but they will be effective. You'll learn to follow through by using action instead of throwing words at your dog. Using the Pup Parenting Plan makes big problems smaller and difficult situations simpler by allowing you to take a step back so you can see the whole picture, and then find a solution.

Before you start using the plan, ask yourself whether you think your dog is the problem. If your answer is yes, remind yourself that almost *all* canine kid problems are created by their human parents. That's good news, because once you change yourself, your dog will change right along with you—for the better.

How do you know where to begin changing yourself? It's easy. First you have to know what you are doing wrong. If you think about a situation you have with your dog that you aren't happy with, read more about each of the mistakes in this chapter. We're sure you'll figure out where you need to focus your work. Even though you probably would prefer jumping right in to fix things, we believe you'll have more success if you can first pinpoint the problem.

FOUR COMMON PUP PARENTING MISTAKES

1. Being reactive instead of proactive

2. Being disrespectful

3. Using punishment

4. Talking too much

Being Reactive Instead of Proactive

The first parenting mistake—being reactive—is the most common. The correction is to become proactive. Think about it. How often do you continue repeating the same problems and the same solutions over and over and over, even if they aren't working, instead of sitting down and thinking about another way to do things? If you're like most parents, you wait till problems occur and then react to them in the moment, which is the time when it is the hardest to make good decisions. Hitting, yelling, threatening, or using your "angry" voice are all reactive; even though they may stop a behavior for a moment, usually, the problem behavior will return. Proactive parents think about what kind of relationship they'd like to have with their dog and then learn ways to make it happen. Proactive parents have the big picture in mind; reactive parents are looking for the quick fix, not worrying about the long-term results.

Reactive doggy parents love to spoil their babies, regardless of the consequences, and the "babies" seem to take to the special treatment without a fight. Proactive, responsive parents know that doggy pampering can become a problem down the road, where they'll end up in a relationship with their four-legged kid that is disrespectful to the dog, themselves, or others.

Being proactive, however, is easier said than done. It doesn't come naturally. Most of you grew up watching your parents react, and you tend to do the same when you're stressed. Many of the dog training manuals recommend reactive training methods, so you may have to unlearn something you're used to and replace it with a new way to parent. If you would like improvement to be long-term, you'll be better off with some advance planning instead of a crisis-by-crisis management approach.

Are you a reactive pup parent? Is this the mistake you need to work on with your dog?

Being Disrespectful

The second mistake pup parents make is being disrespectful to themselves, their pups, or others. Most parents never plan to be disrespectful—it just happens. Respect is the opposite of disrespect, but few pooch parents think about what *respect* really means. Respecting yourself means knowing that you have rights and that it is okay to take care of your needs. Respect for others means that having a dog doesn't give you carte blanche to put friends and family through hardship; they may not love your dog the way you do. Surprisingly, sometimes the most difficult part of the respect piece is understanding your dog's needs. Dogs have two basic needs:

1. The clear definition, from the beginning, of his position as a family member

2. His dependence on his human family members to ensure his well-being by fulfilling his physical, emotional, and psychological needs

Physical needs include feeding him properly, taking care of his health (including his teeth), and engaging in regular exercise. *Emotional needs* include giving him a sense of security, being consistent in your interaction with him, ensuring his need to belong by giving him the opportunity to repay you by serving and pleasing, and acknowledging his devotion with love and appropriate affection. *Psychological needs* include establishing a system of communication with consistent cues and words that your dog can understand, teaching him consistent behavioral standards to enable him to optimally cope with his environment, and carrying out his training in a pleasant and efficient way based on the concepts of mutual respect and trust.

More often than not, the problem with dog rearing is an inability to meet basic needs due to a lack of information or unrealistic expectations. Some people think their dogs will be miserable if they don't get to sleep in their beds or eat people food from the best butcher shops, cooked lovingly by them, or if they have to spend time in a crate or kennel. Some pooch parents give their dogs sugar treats or leave the sliding door to the outside open all day so the dog won't feel hemmed in. There are those who let their dogs roam without a leash and walk amongst the neighbors' gardens so she doesn't get bored. And then there are those families that completely entrust the well-being of their dogs to the children because, after all, the kids promised they would do everything in order to get a dog. We know people who insist their dogs watch Animal Planet all day because they are convinced it is their dog's favorite show. Some dog parents even insist on color-coordinated clothing and designer beds.

You know that dogs don't really need all of these things, but many well-intentioned dog parents consider them necessities. You may enjoy dressing your dog up in outfits that match yours, and a day of Animal Planet viewing never hurt any dog, but we're pretty sure you realize it's a choice, and that your dog doesn't *need* a Hermès scarf or the TV tuned to a particular channel. Too often, misunderstanding your dog's needs (such as thinking she needs sweet treats) can actually be disrespectful to your dog. Have you been a disrespectful pup parent without even realizing it?

Using Punishment

The third mistake pup parents make is using punishment instead of nonabusive, nonpunitive methods to discipline and train their dogs. Hundreds of research projects have demonstrated that punishment is not the most effective way to teach positive outcomes. Then why would so many pooch parents use punishment? Simple. They believe it works and that they are *doing something* instead of allowing their dog to misbehave. One frustrated doggy mom screamed commands at her dog from a block away while he frolicked in the tall grass, completely ignoring her. Would you come to someone who was screaming threats at you? Probably not, and neither would your dog. Yet the woman kept shouting orders because she was exasperated and angry that her dog refused to listen to her and do as she asked.

Others use punishment because they are conditioned from past experiences and lack the knowledge and skills to use different methods. The popular training techniques of the seventies and eighties were based on the following: be the boss, dominate your dog, scruff shake, growl, alpha roll him, stare him down, and use similar confrontational techniques. These methods, aside from being punitive, abusive, and disrespectful, were never particularly effective and in some cases even intensified the problem. Consider Mary, who, upon receiving advice that huskies are pack animals and need to be shown who's the boss, bit her two-year-old female's ear—only to be bitten back, leaving her lip permanently scarred. Very little constructive learning can be done with anger and the output of negative energy.

Many pup parents use punishment because it gives them a sense of being in control—especially when the punishment temporarily stops the problem. They don't want to be permissive and think the only alternative is punishment. When these parents step back and take an objective look, they notice that they are punishing the same behavior over and over again. That is a pretty good clue that punishment doesn't work in the long-term. If this description fits you, you'll be happy to know that you'll learn many respectful discipline methods that are neither punitive nor permissive.

Still other parents use punishment because they are responding to human nature to take the path of least resistance. Further, it is almost impossible to break an old habit until you have something new to replace it. Ever try to quit smoking or lose weight? The human mind abhors a vacuum. It's easier to start something new than to stop something you are used to and replace it with— nothing. Kind and firm pup parenting invites *nonpunitive* and *nonabusive* methods of doggy discipline. Is this the area you need to work on with your dog?

Talking Too Much

You cannot be a calm, authoritative leader with your dog if you are indulging in the fourth mistake that parents make—talking too much. Instead, parents need to talk less and act more. Both canine kids and human kids tune you out when you use too many words. They quickly learn to differentiate when you're talking and when you're acting. They become experts at listening to what we call the tongue in your shoe. The tongue in your mouth makes a lot of noise, but the tongue in your shoe is what we call *action-based follow-through*. It shows your true intention, and kids and dogs pick up when you mean business.

The woman who was screaming commands to her dog from a block away needed to realize that her dog had no idea what she wanted when she unleashed a string of words at him. Even if the dog wanted to please Mom, what was he really supposed to do when he heard, "Come, stay, sit, stop, now, stop, come, lay down"? Action-based follow-through involves making sure you have your dog's attention and then, and only then, giving a directive that your dog can follow and you can carry out. In the case of the frustrated doggy mom, what worked was for her to sit on a park bench holding a treat in her hand, waiting calmly for her dog. When he came, she clipped on his leash, petted him, saying, "Good job. That's a boy," and gave him the treat. She also realized that she needed to make a change and not take her dog off the leash until she had done a better job training herself and her dog.

Are you a pup parent who thinks first, says what you mean, and then follows through with action? Or are you more inclined to talk, talk, talk instead of act, act, act?

A Plan to Combat the Mistakes You Make

Now that you are aware of the four common pup parenting mistakes that create most problems, you are ready to learn about the Pup Parenting Plan. Once you learn this five-step plan, you'll be able to apply it to just about any problem you are experiencing with your dog. We suggest that you use the plan when you've had time to cool down and you aren't right in the middle of a dilemma.

THE PUP PARENTING PLAN

1. Identify the behavior that bothers you.

2. Understand why change is needed.

3. Recognize the mistake you are making.

4. Create a list of possible solutions.

5. Choose a solution and follow through.

The first two steps in the box above are pretty simple. All you have to do is remind yourself what behavior bothers you. Write it down. Then think about why change may be needed and write that down for Step 2. Is the problem dangerous, where either you, your dog, or someone else might get hurt? Is the problem simply annoying and taking away from enjoying your pup? Is the problem stopping you from being your dog's best friend? Is the problem leading to abuse as it gets worse? It helps to be specific when writing about why change is needed.

The third step might be a tough one for you if you don't believe mistakes are opportunities to learn and to try again. Also, it can be difficult to be objective about your own behavior. If you're not sure which mistake you are making, ask someone who knows you. We're pretty sure they'll be able to identify what you need help with!

Step 4 gets easier as you come across the many suggestions for solutions in this book. As you find solutions to some of the problems you're experiencing, write them down. You can add to your list of suggestions by brainstorming with other pooch parents to learn methods that have been effective for them—so long as they are respectful. That last step, choosing a solution and following through, will lead you to success. What follows is how four pup parents used these steps to correct the mistakes they were making.

Reactive Pup Parents Deal with Their Unruly, Ill-Mannered Dog

Scott and Sue were frustrated because their three-year-old golden retriever, Bear, played "catch me if you can"—and they couldn't. They were so exhausted from his games of chase (who wouldn't be after three years?), they were ready to put him up for adoption. If you were a mouse in the corner, you'd notice that Scott and Sue reacted to everything Bear did. It was almost as if they waited for him to misbehave and then attempted to train him using a string of words and commands. They'd yell, beg, plead, threaten, repeat themselves, and promise bribes.

As you might expect, Bear didn't listen to a word they said. He grabbed food off the counters, ran across their new bedspread with muddy paws, and shot out the door the minute it was opened. The worse he got, the more they reacted. Bear was parenting Scott and Sue, and they weren't happy with his parenting style!

Scott and Sue had created the problems they were having with Bear by being reactive parents. Their form of reaction was throwing more words at a situation. They're in good company! We've noticed that parents who react tend to spend a lot of time immobile. It's obvious that they aren't going to take action because they are usually sitting or laying down or shouting commands from another room. Any dog worth his or her salt knows you don't mean business when you're in a resting position or out of eyesight.

Many pup parents, just like Sue and Scott, react with the hope that eventually their dog will get the picture. If they gave the situation a little thought, they'd realize that they are having the same problem over and over; they *could* prepare for it and be ready to take it on by having a plan. That's what Scott and Sue did. They decided to try out the Pup Parenting Plan. They put Bear on a leash, put the leash under the leg of a table, and sat down with paper and pencil to make a plan. Here's what it looked like.

1. The behavior that bothers us: Our dog keeps running away from us in the house and in our fenced-in yard,

and he constantly gets into things. He doesn't listen or respond to our requests or cues. We sometimes think of him as the "golden retriever from Hell."

2. Why change is needed: The situation is annoying, destructive, and could become dangerous if someone leaves the gate open and Bear runs out into the street. We no longer enjoy having a dog. We're as frustrated as we could be.

3. The mistake we are making: We're probably talking too much, but after looking at the common mistakes, we realize that we don't have a plan, either. We are always reacting to Bear's behavior.

4. A list of possible solutions:

- We could close the doors to rooms we don't want the dog to be in. Bear does not need the run of the house.

- We could keep Bear on his leash in the house and tie the end of his leash to the leg of the dining room table. (This solution is further described in Chapter 3.)

- We could try saying "uh-uh" instead of "no," since "no" has completely lost all meaning for Bear because of our overuse and lack of follow-through. We could say it once and then follow through by closing doors and by never leaving a tempting loaf of fresh bread or roast in jumping distance of the dog, who can easily remove the food from the cabinet when we aren't looking. We could also put him in his kennel.

- We could stop giving cues we can't enforce. When we say something, we could use a pleasant voice and say it once, then follow up with action instead of more words.

- We could stop chasing Bear, unless it's playtime outside where we can run and chase each other.

- We could keep Bear in a kennel at home and take him out on a leash to play and exercise.

- We could enroll in obedience training with Bear so we could all learn to use appropriate behaviors.

5. Choose a solution and follow through: Say things once in a pleasant voice and follow up with action.

What worked for Scott, Sue, and Bear

Scott and Sue already spent a lot of time walking with Bear and playing with him at the dog park. They didn't feel comfortable using a kennel, even though they were assured Bear would get used to it and like it. They avoided obedience training because they thought that golden retrievers were by nature very agreeable and easy to handle and didn't need the class. As they mulled over their list of choices, they picked the one that they could consistently enforce instead of reacting to Bear—say things once in a pleasant voice and follow up with action.

They added a special twist to the plan. Scott and Sue knew that Bear loved Rollover, a salami-like dog treat. They agreed to keep a supply in their pockets at all times so they could be ready for Bear. The minute he got the look in his eyes that said, "Let the games begin," Scott or Sue agreed that they would stand *quietly* and say *once* in a kind and soft voice, "Bear, right here." Each time Bear came, they would pet him and tell him how great he was and show him love. Then, they would give him a small piece of Rollover.

They worked with Bear in their living room, with the door closed to the rest of the house. If he didn't come immediately, they stood quietly, Rollover in hand, and waited. After the first request, it took a minute for Bear to come. The second one took fifteen seconds. After that, they hardly got the word "Bear" out of their mouths and he was standing in front of them, waiting for his Rollover.

The first day, Bear gave them many opportunities to practice their solution choice. They stuck to their guns, keeping their voices and body signals happy, enthusiastic, and praising. By the second day, they opened the door from the living room, giving Bear more room to roam. Bear seemed to improve his hearing immensely. It was obvious that Bear associated being called with something very pleasant and delicious. Within a few days, Bear seemed to be perking up his ears, listening carefully and running to his parents at the *first* sound of his name, no matter where they were located.

If Bear could talk, what would he say about this problem? "It's about time my folks took charge. It was exhausting being that out of control. Getting treats for doing what I'm supposed to do is lots more fun than that silly 'catch me' game."

A Family of Four Replaces Disrespect with Respect

Another family dealt with a very familiar pup parenting issue, one that is as old as the ages: their children begged for a dog. The parents said, "Only if you promise to take care of it. You must promise to feed it, give it water, make sure it gets plenty of exercise, and play with it."

The kids said, "Oh, we promise! We promise!"

You know the rest of the story. The kids kept their promise for about a week. Then the hassles began. The kids didn't remember to feed, water, or play with the dog. Their parents nagged, threatened, and punished. They thought of giving the dog away, but by then, they were as attached to the dog as the kids were. They settled for threatening to give the dog away, but the kids didn't believe them. Clearly, there were several problems they were dealing with.

When Tom and Karen took a step back to figure out why change was needed, they reexamined their basic premise—that the kids should keep their promise and take care of the dog. They realized that Nora and Gwen made a promise they couldn't keep, and they had settled for magical thinking instead of dealing with the realities of being a pup parent. Tom and Karen wanted their children to learn how to keep their commitments and be responsible, but they also knew their attempts to teach these important skills by nagging, threatening, and punishing weren't working.

When they examined the kind of mistake they were making, they had to admit that they weren't being respectful to their kids, the kids weren't respecting them, and their miniature schnauzer, Max, was being disrespected by everyone because his basic needs for care weren't being met. Obviously, Max wasn't capable of feeding, walking, and watering himself. They needed a plan.

When Karen and Tom used the Pup Parenting Plan, they involved the children in creating routines for taking care of the dog because they knew that kids are much more willing to follow plans they help create. They had no trouble agreeing that the problem was one of disrespect to Max, whose basic needs weren't being met. They all decided they would like to be better doggy parents. When it came time to brainstorm options, the family came up with a lot of choices, all of which were respectful, *nonpunitive*, and action-based. Here's their list of possible solutions:

- Create a rotation plan that involves each member of the family taking turns meeting Max's needs. Make a chart that shows the days for each person's turn. Instead of nagging, ask Nora and Gwen to look at the chart and answer, "Whose turn is it today?"

- Take the lead from the dog. When Max is howling, pushing his dog bowl around, or looking sad, ask the girls, "What do you think he is trying to tell us?" Trust that one of them will take pity and feed him.

- Just before dinner, draw straws to see who pulls the short straw and "gets" to feed the dog.

Respectful Solutions Eliminate Nagging, Blaming, and Arguing

You'll notice that none of the possible solutions include punishment; Max was a very lucky dog because his family picked the rotation idea and it worked really well. Karen, Tom, Gwen, and Nora created a chore wheel using two paper plates. The larger outside plate had each of the family member's names on it, and the smaller inside plate included a picture (taken by a Polaroid camera) of each chore—one of which was a picture of Max eating his food next to his filled water bowl. Another chore was a set of pictures showing someone letting Max out in the morning and letting him back in. Another picture was of both kids picking up poop in the back yard. (They thought it was great fun doing this for a picture.) The last picture showed one of the girls playing catch with Max. In the center of the wheel they decided to paste a picture of the whole family going for a walk with the dog. Then they attached a brad to the middle of the plates so the kids could rotate the inner plate each day, thus changing which chore would be theirs for that day.

The children did follow through with this chosen plan—most likely because they were respectfully involved in the brainstorming for suggestions and in choosing the one they would use.

If the chore wheel appeals to you, use your imagination *and* your camera. Some families add chores such as brushing the dog's teeth, bathing or brushing the dog, and vacuuming dog hair off the couch.

> If Max could talk, he'd probably say, "I hope they hurry up and decide whose turn it is to feed me. I'm hungry, and I don't really care who feeds me as long as I get fed. Maybe if I sit here looking real hungry, everyone will feed me and I'll have four dinners!"

Punishment Is Not the Answer

Some people mistakenly think that kind and firm solutions reward their dogs for bad behavior and that the only way a dog can learn is to suffer. More often than not, the "solution" for the dog's misbehavior is really misplaced anger or a desire to hurt the dog for hurting you. That's what happened with Francie, who left her new puppy Cody, an American Eskimo dog (a very attached breed who needs attention), home alone for long hours while she went to work. Her little dog was bored and teething, so he entertained himself by chewing on Francie's shoes. Little did he know that his entertainment would make his mom so angry. When Francie walked in and saw one of her $200 shoes in Cody's mouth, she saw red. She pulled the shoe away from him and hit him with it over and over, yelling, "No, no, no! Bad dog, bad dog!" Cody slunk away with his tail between his legs and hid under a chair. Francie grabbed him and threw him outside saying, "You think about what a bad boy you've been." Right!

If Francie thought her methods would stop Cody from chewing on her shoes because she "taught him a lesson," she was soon disabused of the notion when, the next day, he chewed another pair of her best shoes. No amount of yelling and hitting seemed to get through to the little pup.

The Pup Parenting Plan was very simple for Francie.

1. The behavior that bothers me: Chewed up shoes.

2. Why change is needed: Shoes are expensive and I can't afford to keep replacing them.

3. The mistake I am making: Every one of them. I am reactive, disrespectful, punitive, and I talk too much. When she stepped back and looked at the problem objectively, she knew that chewing a shoe is not bad behavior. It is normal dog behavior. The faulty behavior is leaving the shoe in the dog's reach in the first place. Francie could see that it does not make sense to punish

a dog for normal dog behavior, nor does it make sense to assume a dog will learn from punishment. Have you noticed that most pooch parents initially respond just the way Francie did? They punish their dogs for chewing the shoe instead of simply removing their shoes from the dog's path.

4. A list of possible solutions: I don't have to brainstorm for a list of solutions. It's obvious that I must keep my shoes out of sight and provide appropriate chew toys. Instead of brainstorming, she acted:

   - She went to the store and found a shoe rack that hung on the back of her closet door and put all of her shoes in the rack.

   - She also bought a lot of soft stuffed animals at the secondhand store and set them out for Cody to chew. Each animal cost 50 cents—a bargain compared to her shoes. Francie tried rawhide strips, but Cody never liked chewing on them. He preferred something soft, like the shoes, so the stuffed animals were a great substitute and a much better solution than releasing all one's anger at a dog.

5. Choose a solution and follow through: Having a well-thought-out plan made it easy for Francie to follow through. She kept her shoes out of Cody's sight, and she never lost another shoe.

Try to imagine what your dog is thinking while being swatted with the shoe. Do you think he is thinking, "Thank you for caring about me so much that you want to hurt me to teach me right from wrong"? It is more likely that your dog is hurt and totally confused—but amazingly, still loves you.

Francie didn't feel good about hitting Cody and yelling at him. She shook her head at how much she and Cody had suffered because she didn't take the time to think the problem through.

She liked herself a lot better when she was less angry and had a respectful plan. Kind and firm proactive pooch parenting was much more her style.

> *If Cody could talk, what would he say? "I loved the game that Francie used to play with me. I would chew her shoe, she would give me lots of attention, I got to go outside and play in the yard, and when I came back in, she had already left another shoe for me to chew. Oh well, now I have my own special toys to play with."*

All Talk and No Action Creates Sleepless Nights for Newlyweds

Bette and Bob didn't think they would have any problems when they allowed Buster the rottweiler puppy to sleep in their bed. They didn't realize that once Buster grew up and weighed one hundred pounds, his favorite sleeping position would be crosswise, between them. As they clung to separate sides of the bed night after night, they knew they had to take drastic measures.

Like Bette and Bob, many parents don't want their little puppy (or baby) to feel any discomfort at all. Thus begins the "spoiling process" in the name of love or *need*. This newly married couple made the mistake of thinking their little rottweiler pup needed to join them in bed so he wouldn't feel left out. And when Buster was a tiny little puppy, he looked so cute trying to jump up to join them on the bed, they couldn't resist giving him his way. Months later, the hundred-pound dog owned the bed and Bette and Bob were walking around in an exhausted daze.

You've heard the expression "ready, willing, and able," right? Sometimes pup parents are ready, and they're even able, but they aren't willing to do what it takes to create long-lasting change. If you think about it, you probably aren't at your best in the middle of the night, either. Isn't it easier to roll over and go back to sleep than to follow through on a plan? That's what Bette and Bob were doing, until going back to sleep was happening only for their dog. Every night they would make a plan that involved taking turns throwing Buster out of bed. Every night, when Buster started whining, they would turn over, let him back in the bed, and go back to sleep. They didn't follow through. They meant well, but without action, nothing was getting better. They needed to set aside their needs in the short run to have a better behaved pooch (and more rest) in the long run.

If you've started a habit with your pup that you'd like to break, you can benefit from the work that Bette and Bob did. Here's how they used the Pup Parenting Plan.

1. **The behavior that bothers us:** Will we harm our dog or make him feel abandoned and neglected if he doesn't sleep in our bed?

2. **Why change is needed:** Neither of us has had a good night's sleep since we got Buster. He whines and whimpers and barks until one of us, in exhaustion and aggravation, lets him jump up onto the bed. He's the only one who gets to sleep.

3. **The mistake we're making:** We are being disrespectful to ourselves and building resentment and anger toward Buster, who is learning to use whining and barking to control us. He seems content, but we are not. We make plans and we don't follow through, but hey, let's cut us some slack. It's the middle of the night, after all, and we're bushed.

4. **A list of possible solutions:**

   - We could remember that weaning is never easy and that change takes time. We could put in earplugs and let Buster whine and howl, but not let him in our bed. We could trust that, in a few days, he'll get used to sleeping on his new dog bed at the foot of our bed. We can help each other be strong and agree that we'll try this for four nights in a row without weakening.

- We can let Buster sleep in the laundry room until he gets used to sleeping somewhere other than in our bed. We can provide him with a comfortable dog bed and a bowl of water.

- We can inform and/or pass out earplugs to all our neighbors, saying, "Please bear with us. We're trying to teach Buster to stay out of our bed." That way we wouldn't be tempted to let Buster in bed with us because we think he's bothering the neighbors.

- We could get a crate for Buster, keep it in our bedroom, and put him in it when it's bedtime.

- We could get a bigger bed.

- We could put Buster on a four-foot tie-down in our bedroom and position it where he can't jump up onto the bed. (More on the tie-down in Chapter 5.)

5. Choose a solution and follow through: Bette and Bob decided to go for their first choice and let Buster cry and whine, but not let him on the bed when he did. They added one other piece that seemed to comfort everyone. They agreed to take turns sitting next to him on the floor by his bed for four days, petting and soothing him during the night as needed.

It wasn't easy getting up in the middle of the night to do this, but knowing that they were only going to do this for four days helped. Both parents followed through when it was their turn, sitting on the floor next to Buster, petting him and saying in a soothing voice, "There, there, there," until he went back to sleep. And sleep on his own bed he did.

It took three nights of whining before Buster learned that his parents loved him enough to say what they meant and mean what they said. The payoff was that his parents became much more loving when they got rid of all that resentment. And Buster still got to sleep in the same room, but in his very own space!

If Buster could talk, what would he say? "If Mom and Dad thought about this for a minute, they'd realize I sleep all day long when they are not home, and I have no problem sleeping by myself."

Needs Versus Wants

It is important and respectful to meet your kids' needs (both human and canine), but it can be destructive in the long-term to cater to their every want. Did Buster the rott need to sleep in bed with his owners to be fulfilled and loved? Of course not.

You've seen how giving in to your dog or feeling sorry for her often leads to bigger problems down the road. To be your dog's best friend and a savvy pooch parent, you need to consider the long-term effects of your behavior. It is easier to train your dog from the start than to undo bad habits later. But don't fret, because, as we said, it's never too late to teach an old (or young, for that matter) dog new tricks, even when that "dog" might be you. It may take a little time to break bad habits, but you're usually pretty motivated once you experience the disastrous effects of your counterproductive dog-rearing techniques.

Most people don't set out to hurt their dogs or themselves. But many a bad habit, especially a lack of follow-through, gets started when parents don't understand the difference between wants and needs. Giving a dog everything he wants can be very harmful to him in the long run—and can make your life miserable once that "want" becomes a habit. Savvy pup parents find it easier to follow through with their dogs when they know the difference between wants and needs.

Ready to give the Pup Parenting Plan a try? If you haven't done so already, take out that pen or pencil and a pad of paper. Write down the steps and give the plan a try for one of your problems. You might surprise yourself with the options for kind and firm parenting that you are already seeing.

KIND AND FIRM PUP PARENTING PRINCIPLES

1. If your dog is misbehaving, step back and ask yourself if you are being reactive, disrespectful, punitive, or talking too much and acting too little.

2. Don't try to solve problems in the middle of the muddle. Wait till you can give the matter your full attention and then make a plan.

3. Review your dog's basic needs and then remind yourself that you have needs, too.

4. Replace punishment with calm, quiet, and friendly corrections.

5. Use the Pup Parenting Plan to create a strategy that will bring you confidence and success.

6. Use the tongue in your shoes (show your dog how to succeed) instead of the tongue in your mouth (talking too much).

CHAPTER 3

PRACTICAL CONCERNS FOR PUP PARENTS: THE FOUR *L*s

"Not only do animals learn, but the process of learning is pretty much the same whether you're a pigeon, a planarian or, come to think of it, a philosophy professor."

—*Patricia B. McConnell, PhD*, Bark *magazine*

You fall in love with a puppy. Your kids beg for a dog and you don't want to say no to them. You had a great dog when you were a kid and you feel empty without one. Your heart goes out to a mutt in the shelter. You've always had dogs and you don't feel complete without one. This is all fine. Love is an important factor when adding a dog to the family. However, to create a respectful family relationship that includes a dog, there are many practical issues to consider.

In the following chapters, you'll see how love of your dog helps you deal with the special needs of parenting a puppy. Love will help you take the time that is needed to learn to communicate better with your dog. You'll be motivated to use effective methods, such as cues and set-ups, to get your dog's attention. You'll find that love for your dog can be shared by an entire support network to help you parent your pooch. Love will also help you during those times when things go terribly wrong.

But love can only go so far when it comes to practicalities; in addition to love, you need to consider the more realistic aspects of pup parenting. Even though it seems obvious to think about your lifestyle, living space, phase of life, and money, most pup parents don't think these things through. We call these the Four *L*s of Pup Parenting: *Lifestyle*, *Living Space*, *Life Phase*, and *Loot*. Focusing on these Four *L*s will help you strengthen your practical side when deciding what kind of dog to add to your family or figuring out how to repair any damage that has already been done.

Take a minute and think about which of the Four *L*s most applies to your situation. If you are curious, read more about each of the *L*s. If you'd like help with a specific situation, find that section and read it with care. You may be surprised at how many simple answers to seemingly complex problems you'll find.

> *If interviewed for an opinion on the Four Ls, we think dogs would say: "The next time you get that look in your eye like you're planning to get rid of me, I'd just like to remind you that **you** chose **me.**"*

Pup Choices Should Reflect Your Lifestyle

Lifestyle describes what your days look like and how you spend your time. Give it some thought. What kind of lifestyle do you lead? Travel-heavy? Avid jogger? *Brady Bunch* brood? Single parent? Workaholic with a two-hour commute? Starving student? And where do you live? In the country on a ranch? In a cozy apartment where dogs over twenty-five pounds are forbidden? In a high-rise building where it can be a hassle to deal with elevators every time your dog needs to go outside? In a house with a fenced-in yard?

Imagine how your lifestyle will affect the amount of time your dog will need to spend alone. Will you have the time to train, teach, and play with your dog? Do you really know how much love and attention your dog will need? Do you have a support network of friends and other family members who will help you during emergencies? Have you got a plan for your pup when you travel?

Did you really think about all this when your kids were pulling you toward the pet store window, begging for that puppy? Pup parents must find ways to adjust their lifestyle to accommodate their "baby." Just how much are you willing to change your lifestyle for a canine family member?

Some people might find the following story excessive, but it happens to be true. It didn't surprise us, though, as we know many pup parents who would do exactly the same thing for the welfare and happiness of their canine kid. A couple sold their third-floor condo with a beautiful view of the San Francisco Bay and moved to a smaller townhouse without the view because it was too much trouble to take the elevator up and down to walk their dogs and because they wanted a yard for their dogs to play in. With some advance thought and planning about their lifestyle with dogs, they might have purchased a different condo in the first place—or waited until a later stage in their lives to have a dog. Once they had their dogs, however, they decided to adjust their priorities— and their dogs won. They moved.

There are so many things to think about before bringing a dog home to live with you: traveling with them, grooming, and personality (yours and your pup's), to name a few. Consider the following:

TRAVEL: If you often travel by plane, whether for pleasure or to hop between homes, consider finding a dog, such as a toy poodle, that would be comfortable in a carrier case that can fit under the seat in front of you. She will be a lot easier to manage than, say, a St. Bernard, who would have to travel "cargo class."

DAILY CARE: Some dogs are very high maintenance, so you might want to think twice before choosing a dog that has to be brushed daily, such as an Afghan hound, regardless of whether he'll ever see the show ring. On the other hand, this could be a great hobby if you have retired and are looking for a full-time activity.

TEMPERAMENT: Some breeds—you know the ones—make for great guard dogs, but if you have small children, you'd probably want to seriously think about this before getting a dog that has guarding tendencies; they might snap at or bite kids who go near their food. Dalmatians love to run and play and need a tremendous amount of exercise. If you lead a quiet, peaceful lifestyle, counting spots on your dog won't be enough to keep his high-energy highness happy. You will, however, get more exercise cleaning up dog hair from this shedding breed.

COST: If you have trouble hanging onto money or are trying to build that nest egg, we don't recommend breeds like bulldogs or shar-pei, even if you think they are the cutest dogs in the world. They tend to have a lot of medical problems that could cost you a fortune.

AGE: They may be irresistibly cute (take another look at the cover), but puppies require your full attention for potty training, comfort, play, and exercise. If you work full-time or you're often otherwise gone for ten hours at a time, with no one at home to keep the "baby" company, you might be better off with a goldfish.

Get the picture?

A lot of folks don't think about any of these lifestyle issues when they add a dog to their family. Ron and Lisa are an extreme example of future parents who indulged in magical thinking instead of realizing the particulars about their lifestyle. Lisa followed her heart instead of her head when she attended a charity auction and brought home a chocolate Labrador for $1,000. The sale may have broken all records for the event, but the choice was a poor one. As the gavel slammed down, and the auctioneer rambled on about the record sale of the evening, Ron looked at Lisa and shook his head in disbelief. "You've certainly done it this time, honey. How are you planning to take care of a puppy with your work schedule? I hope you don't think I'll be training this guy."

Lisa was in denial, like a lot of pup parents are when they add a dog to the family. She told Ron, "Don't be a wet blanket. I've had dogs since I was a kid. All they need is a big back yard and two squares a day, a little petting, and clean water. (In your dreams, Lisa!) And think of how much money we just donated to a great cause."

Lisa made an impulse decision to bring a new family member into her life, one that she would be responsible for the next twelve to eighteen years. If you have acted like Lisa, it's not too late to make up for your mistake. That little pup needs you to be a responsible parent. If you are willing to make the shift, you can redeem your impulse decision by becoming more realistic. If you don't want to do that, you'll probably end up like Lisa did.

She wasn't interested in becoming a doggy parent; Lisa was more focused on the role of Lady Bountiful. As a result, the dog suffered from a lack of training and attention. He was undisciplined and created chaos in her house, eating her new cashmere sweater and three new pairs of shoes, chewing on her furniture, ruining her carpet, and tearing up the backyard. Nine months later, Lisa found a new family for her dog—one that was willing to take on the responsibility of doggy parenting.

Does Your Dog Need a Playmate?

Many pooch parents think that getting a playmate for the dog will solve their lifestyle problems if they have to spend a lot of time away from home. They hope that by keeping each other company, the two dogs will train each other to behave. If you are thinking your first dog will take your place as trainer, or that your second dog will take your place as companion, think again. Even though dogs can learn a lot from each other and enjoy each other's company, dogs can't have another dog as a pet.

Both of your dogs need you as their primary influence. It's your job to assume responsibility and leadership with the second dog as well as the first. You need to be the primary teacher, spending as much time as necessary with each dog to help him learn what is expected and how to belong.

Dogs, like children, need quality time with their parents. We recommend spending special time alone with each dog as well as time with them together. Obedience training should be done on a one-on-one basis, including practice walks. You can take both dogs when walking for fun, exercise, and relaxation (even though, on occasion you might have to put up with tangled leashes along the way).

We're not saying that you should avoid adding a second dog to your family; we are advising that you just be more realistic about what the choice means. When Grant and Katie decided to look for a second dog, they did so because they thought their mastiff, Reginald, needed company. Their main criterion was to make sure the new dog fit in the back seat of the car with Reginald. A friend had an adorable miniature schnauzer whose mother had recently delivered another litter. The dog seemed like it would be the perfect size for the family car. Upon seeing the schnauzer pup at the breeders, Grant and Katie added several more "good" reasons for selecting the dog: it would be fun to have a light dog and a dark dog, a big dog and little dog, a guard dog and a lap dog. Grant and Katie were leading with their feelings, not their brains.

Luckily for them, since Reginald was well trained and well behaved, he taught the puppy many good behaviors. Keep in mind, however, that that's not always the case. The second dog is most often younger and will pick up many of your older dog's bad habits. We're not sure whether the reverse is also true when your new dog is an older adoption or rescue. It's been our experience that the dog who lives in the house first is the one to teach the newer dog, young or old, all his tricks. In either case, the second dog will often copy the first dog by observing—we've heard stories of female dogs who learned to lift their legs from a male buddy!

Also keep in mind that two dogs together being left alone in the yard all day very often bark more because of play barking and pack mentality behavior (following the established leader). Two dogs together can re-landscape your yard in a matter of hours. (Just think of what they can do to your house!) Two dogs can also create challenges when riding in the car. Veterinary care, feeding, grooming, and kenneling costs seem to multiply exponentially with two dogs. Be ready for the additional problems of adding a second dog instead of thinking that the decision will be the solution to all your troubles.

Some Lifestyle Changes Are Inevitable

In spite of your best preparations, there may still be times when you have to make sacrifices. Here are some examples we've heard of: The Rodriguez family, used to traveling by plane, decided to take turns going on some of their trips, as they didn't want the dogs going on a plane and they weren't happy leaving them with strangers, no matter how highly recommended they came. The Smith family had to invest in a very expensive heavy-duty vacuum after finding out that two of their six children were allergic to dog hair. The Jordans bought a new car when they discovered that their dog could leap over the front seat and eat anything in sight, including groceries and boxes of Kleenex. Yes, we know they could have used a tie-down system, seat belt, or a gated divider between front and back seats. Maybe they used the dog as an excuse to buy the car they really wanted. At any rate, the list goes on, and we're sure you have a story or two with situations you never dreamt would happen by adding a dog to the family. Dog parents are happiest when their dogs are happy, and they will often make lifestyle changes to accommodate a dog they have fallen in love with.

> If dogs could talk, here's what we think they would say about the first L: "Lifestyle, schmifestyle. Either you're a dog person or you aren't. And if you're a dog person, that's the lifestyle for me."

Dog Proof Your Living Space

Did you know how much you would have to modify your living space to accommodate a dog? If you had known you would need more than a dish, a bag of dog food, a leash, and some toys, would you still have brought your dog home? Probably. But isn't it too bad that no one had a "baby" shower for your new dog, supplying you with the myriad contraptions needed to keep Rover safe and sound? (We wouldn't be surprised if doggy showers soon become an "in" thing.) Spread out over the lifetime of your dog, the resources you spend making your living space safe and dog friendly are small compared to the joys of having a dog in the family. As one couple said, "Our dogs mean everything to us." They could be speaking for a lot of pup parents.

But before bringing your dog home, you might need to check a few assumptions at the doggy door. Eileen Mitchell, who writes the *San Francisco Chronicle* newspaper column "Dog's Life," explains, "No matter how much you adore your pet, one thing is certain: Once you decide to share your home with an animal, you might as well toss that stack of *Town and Country* magazines right into the recycling bin...because no matter how clean and well-trained your pet is, there are still some not-so-lovely things that are unavoidable."

Think about your living space. What's yours like? How well will a dog fit in? Is your house and its contents a large "dog toy" ready to be chewed up when you turn your back? Can it be dog-proofed? Is your outside physical space dog friendly? Can you put your dog outside without worrying about her running away, getting heat stroke, getting dog-napped, or digging up your garden? If not, what needs to be done to make it ready? How big is your car? Do you have neighbors who would be irritated by a barking and/or howling dog? Do you have roommates who may not be as crazy about your dog as you are? Do you live in a high-rise building where you have to take an elevator to get outside with your dog? Many of the issues you may be struggling with now can be resolved by dealing with your living space. It is the easiest of the Four *L*s to correct and organize, and a little bit of effort around living space can create endless freedom for you and your pup.

A Family Dog Belongs with the Family

If you haven't figured it out yet, here's the first big piece of news: Your dog belongs in the house with you. If you are thinking that it's not fair to your dog to keep him in the house because he would be happiest outside all day, we'd like you to reconsider. That may have been the case when dogs lived in an area where they could run around safely without hurting themselves or others, but times have changed. In our society, dogs need to be socialized so they can get along; they need to be kept safe so they don't get injured or killed; and they need to be trained so that when they are in the house they are a welcome part of the family.

Here's another important bit of news: If your dog spends a lot of time outside, not only is he missing socialization and consistency, he is also learning too much independence. He makes up his own rules, which could lead him to think he is setting the culture for the family instead of the other way around. You're the doggy parent, and it's your job to create the family way of life.

Too much backyard time can also create frantic, hectic, over-excitable behavior in dogs. Some pup parents believe frenetic behavior is a sign that their dog is an "outside" dog, thus creating a vicious cycle. These dogs have never been given a chance to learn acceptable social behavior. Then they get yelled at and pushed away the few times somebody does go out in the backyard and gets a dose of the poor dog's needy and desperate attempts to get attention. Consequently, the dog mom or dad decides to spend less time with the dog, who gets less of what he needs. The sad thing is that these dogs are often put down because their parents think the dogs are the problem.

If you have one of these "backyard dogs," you *can* turn your dog into an indoor dog—if you are patient and do the necessary training. If your dog has been outdoors for three or four years, it may be more difficult. On the other hand, you could be pleasantly surprised at how relieved and happy your dog will be and how quickly she will get accustomed to being a house dog.

We realize that people who have hunting dogs might take exception to this information, but even an avid hunter discovered that his German shorthaired pointer, Tucker, seemed to thrive from spending time inside with him. He said, "Tucker is the best hunting dog I've ever had, and I enjoy him more than any of my other dogs. I take him to my work site, he rides everywhere in the car with me, and when I visit my adult kids, he lives inside with us. (But don't tell my wife!)" Your dog is a companion and family member first and foremost.

There are, of course, always exceptions. When they arise, you take your cue from your dog. We've known some dogs who really hate being inside and stand at the door to go out whenever they are in. But that's very different from *you* deciding that your dog's place is outside and never allowing her to be part of the family. These dogs are also well behaved when they are with their pup parents—they simply prefer being outside. Lynn's Samoyed, Buddy, was one of those dogs. As he grew older he created a job for himself: guarding the perimeter. He would stand at the door and howl softly until let out, unless it was raining, thundering, or the Fourth of July.

We've also seen some indoor dogs adjust quite well when faced with outdoor sleeping arrangements. When Hobbs, a vizsla who grew up in a Chicago high-rise, came to spend a month at his country cousins' home in Napa, California, he found that dogs weren't allowed in the house—ever! His mom and dad were worried about whether he could adjust to the outdoors, but after a night of howling out in the rain, he discovered the doghouse and his cousins, two hunting dogs. They welcomed him like an old friend and soon the three were playing together like long-lost friends. When Hobbs's mom and dad go back to Chicago, he'll be back inside, but his "camp out" in the country has suited him nicely.

Aside from these exceptions, most dogs do have very strong social needs, and these include spending the night sleeping inside with their families. The greatest favor you can do a dog is to allow him to share your space with you so he doesn't live the life of an outcast.

Don't panic. We're not saying that keeping your dog inside means allowing him the run of the house. With good reason, you should be horrified with the idea of your dog jumping on the furniture, defecating or urinating on the carpets, or acting wild and crazy. Your dog needs to learn what is and what is not acceptable and not be allowed to think he owns the house and can do whatever he wants whenever he wants. Even though he has a perfect right to share the house with you, his staying inside is based on mutual respect. This means you respect his need for socialization and attention and your need for order and cleanliness.

A lot of people reading this book have dogs who live inside and have never caused problems. If this is you, you have a dog that acclimated to family life and found a special place that worked for everyone. She has her special spot on the couch because that's okay with you or on your kid's bed, where she spends most of her day. Or she sleeps on a rug by the door, waiting for you to come home. She runs in and out because you have a "doggy door" for her to do that. Or you are home all day and your dog hangs out near your feet, especially when you're in the kitchen.

However, you may have a dog that needs more training to adjust to in-home living. What would be your first clue? Suppose you left your dog inside while you were out and about. You came home and discovered that he had pulled all the games off the shelf, scattered the pieces from one end of the room to another, and eaten most of the Monopoly set. Or how about this: While home alone, your dog snuck into the only room in the house with carpet and left you a wet spot and a pile of dog poop. Or think of your own story—we know you've got them. Some dog parents are tempted to ban this type of dog to the outside forever, but we feel that would be a mistake.

The Pup Parenting Plan Can Help Acclimate Your Dog to the House

Perhaps your dog learned some behaviors that were okay as a puppy but that are no longer acceptable once he became fully grown. This was the case with Mary and Mark, who thought it was fun to have Marley on the couch with them when he was a puppy. But when the large black Labrador became full grown and they got a new couch, it wasn't so cute any more. They didn't have any trouble breaking Marley of this habit when they were home; they simply wouldn't let him on the couch. However, they started to suspect Marley was sleeping on the couch when they were gone. One cushion seemed to have more wear and a distinct doggy odor. To check out their suspicions, they left a sticky note on the couch with the sticky part facing up. Sure enough, they came home to find the sticky note on Marley's butt.

Mark smacked the couch hard and said, "Couch! No!" Marley gave him that hangdog, guilty look that only dogs can give. This gave Mark and Mary the impression that Marley *knew* he shouldn't get on the couch, which made them very frustrated because they couldn't keep him off the couch even though he "knew" better.

Here's how the Pup Parenting Plan helped them understand exactly why their communication wasn't working, and how to fix the problem.

1. The behavior that bothers us: Marley won't follow the rules when we're not home to enforce them.

2. Why change is needed: Frankly, we don't like the smell or the fact that our couch is wearing out. We can't afford a new one right now.

3. The mistake we're making: Since Marley doesn't obey, is that a sign that we are talking too much? Probably. Maybe we aren't meeting our dog's basic needs when we expect something of him that he isn't capable of doing (obeying on his own when we're not home). If that is true, we need to follow through in a different way.

4. A list of possible solutions:

   • Give in and let Marley sleep on the couch when we aren't there and start saving for a new couch.

   • Cover the couch with a blanket when we're gone, so Marley can sleep on the blanket.

   • Keep Marley in the back yard when we are gone— even though this can sometimes be for hours.

- Keep Marley in a dog crate. (It is a good thing we are just brainstorming, because we already know we couldn't stand this one.)

- Put up an ex-pen (see page 50 for details) so Marley has to stay in the kitchen area.

- Put something on the couch so he can't get on it.

5. Choose a solution and follow through: Mary and Mark accepted that they couldn't control Marley's behavior when they were away from home, and they decided they had to find a way to protect their couch. They didn't like the idea of a blanket cover, because they knew Marley would pull it off, play with it, and then jump back on the couch. Instead, they looked around their home for something they could lay on the couch when they left for work. It took them only seconds to put a bar stool on the couch just before they left home. They wondered if Marley would figure out how to drag the bar stool off the couch, and were happy to see it was still there when they got home. They wished they had thought sooner of something so simple.

If dogs could talk, we think Marley might say: "Aren't my mom and dad adorable and clever? Good thing they get to practice parenting on me before they have human children."

Setting Up Your Living Space

Without a responsible dog owner, what remains is an "irresponsible" dog. Just as Mark and Mary discovered, there are many ways to help your dog succeed in the house with a little effort on your part. You'll find that potty training is much easier when your dog starts as a house dog. We've covered simple solutions for potty training in Chapter 5. Here, we are focusing on how to set up your living space to make it dog friendly without sacrificing your needs.

Often, the simplest solution is to find a smaller area to confine your dog where she can't get into trouble, get hurt, or destroy the house. Lynn's first dog, Thumper, a Scotty-poo, was kept in the kitchen while he was being potty trained. Lynn remembers laughing when her two-foot-tall dog would stand behind the ten-inch board blocking the doorway. He could easily have climbed over the board, but he was patiently waiting to be allowed to play in the rest of the house.

Similarly, the Richards family kept their poodle, along with a doggy bed, toys, food, and water, in the laundry room when they were away from the house. Often the washer or dryer were running, and the Richards were convinced the sound of the washer and the warmth of the dryer made her happy. The Smiths, on the other hand, let their dog have more freedom, but they used baby gates to block off the second floor. They closed the doors to their first-floor bedroom, office, and bathroom (where their dog couldn't seem to resist eating what was in the garbage can or unrolling the toilet paper roll).

Crate Training and Ex-Pens

A lot of dog parents like using the crate method for training, but it's not for everyone. Crates come in different sizes and are usually made of wire with a soft pad on the bottom. They have a door that closes. We don't like the idea of leaving dogs in crates for long periods of time, but it is recommended by some dog trainers. We prefer ex-pens.

Ex-pens are similar in design to a portable fence that can be purchased with a variety of panels to make it many different sizes. It stands up on its own and allows a place for a dog to be confined while still having room to roam. It can be used inside on any noncarpeted surface. Many dog owners put the dog's food, water, toys, and sleeping bed inside the ex-pen and leave their dogs in the pen while they are at work.

These props are effective when you're at home. The Clarks used an ex-pen to help their giant schnauzer, Ralph, learn to stop begging when they sat down for dinner. Every time Ralph stood at eye level with a family member—with mouth open, panting, and drooling while they ate—they put him in the ex-pen with a baited bone (a hollow bone filled with Ralph's favorite food—peanut butter), saying kindly, "Ralph, you can try again later." Whether Ralph understood the words or not, he got the message to keep his distance from the dinner table.

The Johnsons had another problem. Their cocker spaniel, Sadie, hovered nearby whenever they changed their baby's diaper on the living room floor. It took only one time watching the dog gobble up the baby's bowel movement to motivate them to change the arrangement. They put a leash under the leg of the table (a method called the tie-down system), and when it was time to change the baby, first they snapped the buckle onto Sadie's collar, and then changed the baby safely out of her reach. If this icky-to-humans incident causes you to think that the Johnsons should have known better than to change the baby on the floor, we'd like to remind you that dogs are full of surprises when they act like dogs. Sometimes we humans need a wake-up call to remember that a dog is still a dog. Like many pup parents, the Johnsons had to learn that the hard way.

We've heard of many success stories using the tie-down system. For some dogs, it's easy to train them by snapping their leash onto their collar in the house and letting them roam around with leash dangling. If they get into something they shouldn't, all you have to do is connect the grip end of the leash to an immovable object (like a table leg, chair, or your leg if you are seated) till you are ready to let your dog try again.

> If dogs could talk about living space, we think they might say: "Come on, admit it. Wouldn't you rather have a place that looks a little lived in than live without me?"

Life Phases Make a Difference

Each life phase comes with a different set of issues, behaviors, and feelings. Think of the differences between being a young adult just leaving home and a set of newlyweds; a family with school-age children and empty-nesters; a single career-person and a senior. We encourage you to take your phase of life into consideration when choosing to parent a pup, since it affects your relationship with your dog.

Consider the young adult traveling around the country on a road trip, camping somewhere new each night. Would a dog who had a long coat and picked up burrs and foxtails be a good choice? Probably not. Would a young couple busy with school or work have the time to groom a Bouviers des Flandres or Pekingese? We think that those three to eight hours a week might be better spent on other activities. We hope a family with young children wouldn't choose a dog that has food guarding tendencies or possessive aggression. Imagine the bite marks on the crawling baby who made the mistake of getting too close to the dog's dish or dog's mommy or daddy. Unacceptable! Which dog would be better for a senior who has a hard time walking: a large dog with high energy who requires a long walk each day or a small lap dog who is content to cuddle and sleep most of the day?

We're not implying that there is a right dog for each life stage. Rather, when choosing a dog, a bit of planning based on information about life phases can prevent disasters or worse yet, dogs who must be put down or given away. We highly recommend giving your life phase careful consideration and doing your homework before adding a dog or a particular breed to your life.

The Youthful Parent

Twenty-year-old Peter, a young adult living alone for the first time, wanted a dog for company. After a few years attending the local junior college while living at home, Peter decided to strike out on his own. He moved to the mountains so he could snowboard, climb, and kayak. Like a lot of young people, he quickly discovered that to pursue all his interests, he'd have to live with a lot of roommates and work full-time just to make ends meet. He rented a place with three other roommates and found a job at a local retail outlet. During his free time, he partied, spent time with his girlfriend, and pursued the seasonal sport of his choice. But he felt lonely. He was missing something. That's when he decided to add Nellie, an eight-week-old golden retriever, to his life.

Peter's folks wouldn't let him have a dog while he lived at home, so once he realized he had a few extra dollars at the end of each month, he saved up for Nellie. And to his surprise, Peter took to doggy parenthood like a pro.

Peter lived in a mountain community where dogs were welcome in many stores, so he took Nellie to work every day. She slept in her wire kennel in front of the register counter and entertained the customers with her adorable little snores and paw positions while she slept. When she was awake, Peter let her roam around the small store. Her favorite place was a hideout behind the counter where no one could see her. When there were no customers in the store, Peter brushed Nellie and taught her tricks. By the time she was three months old, she already had a repertoire that delighted Peter and his customers. Each time one of them saw Nellie's kennel and asked about the dog, Peter whistled and out she came, ready to perform her four famous tricks (sit, lay, stay, and roll over).

Peter says that the secret for his success with Nellie is that, in his opinion, dogs needed to be with their parents when they were small, so he took Nellie everywhere. She had a special spot in his truck and her kennel at his work. She even accompanied him when he went kayaking. He bought her a bright red CFD (canine flotation device) to wear until he was sure she was a strong swimmer. Nellie would sit with her nose resting on the side of the kayak, content and calm. Peter also noted that Nellie charmed the socks off his girlfriend and roommates, who played with Nellie and helped Peter out whenever they could.

Contrast this with Dale's situation. Not every young person leaving home is ready to become a dog parent. Dale wanted a big dog to take with him everywhere, sure that girls would be impressed seeing him walking with his large charge. He started researching breeds on the Internet and decided the Alaskan malamute would be perfect for him because it was good looking, highly intelligent, and muscular. Since Dale had his black belt in karate, he knew that he had the strength and agility to train and parent a malamute.

The breeder Dale contacted was a wise man who understood the idiosyncrasies of the breed. He knew the malamute wasn't for everyone, so he recommended that his potential customers spend some time house-sitting or hanging out with malamutes before adding a pup to their family. Dale agreed to house-sit for one of the breeder's previous customers.

After spending a week with a malamute, Dale came to the conclusion that adding a dog to his life would severely cramp his style. Malamutes need a lot of exercise, especially early in the morning; Dale liked sleeping in. Malamutes also shed—*a lot!* Dale liked his clothing and car to be dog-hair free. Malamutes love to dig and howl; Dale had experienced difficulty finding an apartment he could afford and realized that the extra pet security deposit would be out of his reach. Malamutes are also aloof; Dale couldn't afford a place without roommates, and the roommates he had were afraid of the big dog he brought over to visit. The clincher came when Dale realized that his picture of walking with his dog didn't include a leash. Malamutes have a mind of their own when off leash, as Dale found out when the dog ran away and wouldn't come back when called. So much for his romantic fantasies.

The simple act of "trying on" dog parenting saved both Dale and a future dog a lot of trouble. He wasn't ready for a dog. He wasn't settled the way Peter was. Dale was a bit of a dreamer, but by having a chance to try out parenthood, he woke up in a hurry!

The Young Family or Couple

Not everyone gets the chance to "borrow" a dog before adding one to the family. Hundreds of parents of young children bought dogs on impulse after seeing the movie *101 Dalmatians*. The Sylvesters bought a darling puppy without doing a bit of research or advance planning when the two- and four-year-olds begged and begged for the spotted dog. It didn't take them long to discover that dalmatians may not be the best breed for children. They typically have high energy and a mind of their own—they don't care about pleasing you. The Sylvesters' dalmatian, Aspen, was very rambunctious. When the boys tried to play with her, Aspen was too rough. She would knock them down, bite them, and rip their jeans. It didn't take long for the kids to stay as far away from Aspen as they could.

Even though the kids didn't learn to love Aspen at first, Mr. Sylvester did, in spite of her biting and dog hair. Essentially, Aspen became his dog. He was willing to take the time for training and caring for Aspen. As she and the kids grew older, they also bonded and became involved in her care. They love Aspen, but next time they choose a dog, Mr. Sylvester swears he'll take time to research the breed first, and pay more attention to his lifestyle.

Would you now agree with our advice to avoid impulse buying when it comes to adding a dog to your family? Would you at least be willing to sleep on the decision and do a little research before making the choice? We hope so.

Buying on impulse isn't the only life phase problem. How many people choose the same kind of dog they grew up with, only to find that the dog doesn't fit their family circumstances at all? Just because your family always had dachshunds when you were a kid doesn't mean that you want to deal with their frequent bladder and back problems in your family of today. Making a selection based on childhood memories isn't always the best option, especially if your phase of life doesn't leave a lot of extra time for trips to the veterinarian. Remember, the dog you had as a kid was parented by someone other than you. Now that you're the dog parent, be more thoughtful before jumping to a decision.

Young couples come with their own set of issues. First they have to both agree that having a dog is okay; then they need to agree on a dog both will like. Think of the problems that could occur if one person wants a dog and the other hates dogs. It happens. For active young couples, a dog that can keep up is also important. Paul and Paula were newlyweds who wanted to fill out their family by adding a dog they could play with. They weren't ready for children, but they did picture having a dog who would frolic with them at the beach, jog with them on their morning runs through the park, and play fetch in the backyard. A black Labrador seemed like the perfect dog to complete their lifestyle picture. A friend told them they had to get an AKC-registered purebred dog. Since they had never purchased a dog before, they thought their friend knew best. After researching breeders, they found a Lab puppy that stretched their newlywed budget by a whopping $400.

When their black Lab, Bruno, ended up being moody and inactive, Paul and Paula were troubled and disappointed. Weren't Labradors supposed to be high-spirited, playful, and lively? In spite of your best efforts, there is always the chance of ending up with a dog who doesn't fit the characteristics, just like Bruno. What do you do when that happens? By the time Paula and Paul realized Bruno wasn't going to be the dog of their dreams, they were too attached to send him away. Eventually, they added another dog to the family who was much more lively and who encouraged Bruno to be more playful.

The Older Parent

John and Rachael were facing an empty nest, so they started talking about adding a dog to the family. They were looking for the next "kid." What they didn't consider is that neither had been *pup* parents before. Rachael said she wanted to learn more about dogs because she thought they were interesting, and John had dogs as a kid and enjoyed them—if Rachael wanted a dog, that was enough for him. Those were pretty unrealistic expectations to add another living creature to their family.

Upon further discussion, John and Rachael realized that their cats might not take to a dog and that when they relocated after the kids graduated, a dog might not fit into their new lifestyle. They made an excellent decision. Before proceeding and adding a dog to the family, they agreed to house-sit for John's sister to have an opportunity to spend more time with an actual dog. Her dog, Curly, gave them a real education.

John and Rachael were avid hikers and John loved to jog. The first thing they discovered was that Curly didn't walk at their pace. Every time they sped up, Curly slowed down. He'd plant his front paws, lean back, and do a "hockey stop." Rachael and John scratched their collective heads trying to figure out what the dog needed. Eventually, they realized the dog was walking them. It wasn't as easy as it looked to walk a dog.

They did enjoy how undemanding Curly was during the day, as he spent most of it sleeping on his rug. They replaced their fantasy of getting a puppy with a realistic decision to get an older dog, either through a rescue or re-homing organization. At last they found the perfect dog who could not only walk fast, but could keep up with John when he jogged.

Their mixed-breed "mutt," Alfie, bonded with them within weeks, ran three miles a day with John, and slept at his side while he worked in his home office. As for the cats, once the felines let Alfie know who *really* ran the house, the three animals played quite nicely together, much to everyone's amazement.

The Grand-Parent

We recommend that if you're a senior, check out the adult dogs either in animal shelters or through rescue groups. (If you're 80, you wouldn't want a puppy with a life expectancy of 16 years, would you?) If you're looking for a dog to replace one who has died, you may be able to find a dog whose owner has also died or had to go into a convalescent home or is no longer physically capable of caring for a dog. Many Humane Societies and rescue groups provide temporary homes for these dogs who are then available for adoption. It wouldn't be hard for a grieving senior to find a small breed who is four to six years old, in good health, and who has many years left to share with a new pooch parent.

That's what happened to Woody and Agnes. They became pup parents of a little apricot toy poodle, Sadie, when their neighbor had a stroke and had to move to a nursing home. None of her family members were willing to take her dog. Since Woody and Agnes already knew Sadie and were comfortable with her, they decided to offer to take her so she could stay in a place she was familiar with, being around people she knew. Their neighbor left a list of guidelines, so they knew Sadie's routines, what she ate, the name of her veterinarian, what medicine she needed, and what stuffed animals she slept with. That made the transition much easier. (We recommend you keep such a list for your dog just in case of an emergency.)

If Woody and Agnes hadn't taken Sadie, she could have become a rescue dog. People who organize rescue groups are usually animal lovers and are very dedicated to their jobs. Without any compensation, they voluntarily assist other people in either finding dogs or finding homes for dogs. If you know of a dog that needs rescue, or you want to become involved rescuing dogs, call your local SPCA (Society for the Prevention of Cruelty to Animals) or a trainer, or search the Internet for information on Project Breed Rescue, Mixed Breed Rescue, and Hybrid Rescue. These Web sites contain listings of rescue services from all over the United States.

There is another great resource for elderly folks called "Loving for Life." In order to use this service, you must first be a member of the Humane Society and you must also have a clause in your will specifying that you want your dog to belong to the Humane Society when you die. They will guarantee that they will keep the dog and not euthanize your canine kid unless the dog is unhealthy. They also guarantee that they'll find a placement for the dog. The Humane Society also has a free adoption service for seniors to encourage them to take an older dog who may already be used to living with a senior.

Pup parents become very attached to their dogs, so it is important to think about your phase of life when creating a doggy family, doing your best to partner with the right dog for your life phase.

> If dogs could talk, we think they might say this about life phases: "Remember that you're not the only one with life phases. With any luck, you'll enjoy all of our ages and stages and live to be a ripe old age, right along with us."

Loot—It Sure Does Help

If parents really knew the emotional and financial costs of raising a child before they had one, it might be the end of the human race. Those of us who have raised children feel grateful for the opportunity, as do parents of pooches, in spite of the costs. But it does help to know more about loot issues in advance.

For those of you with human children, you've already discovered that the amount of money spent giving birth to your baby was the least amount of money you spent on that child. So it is with dogs. Most likely, the money it takes to purchase your pup will be the smallest amount of money you'll spend on your dog during her lifetime, and for some of you, that amount won't be small. So where does all the other money go? Between necessities, grooming, and veterinary care, it's easy to plunk down around $1,500 a year. That doesn't count the endless dollars you can spend pampering your pooch with high-end luxury items. If it's not too late, it's best to ask yourself how much disposable income you have. Can you really afford a dog? If you already have a dog, you know firsthand how much loot is needed. Shocking, isn't it?

You can flip ahead to Chapter 4 for detailed information on where to buy your dog, but for now, realize that even though the sale price might be a whopper, it's just a shadow of what's to come. You can't even avoid loot challenges by rescuing a dog from the pound; those dogs don't come without a price either.

The list of necessities is long and expensive: crates, fencing, dog food, training equipment, veterinary care, spaying/neutering, shots, flea treatments, heartworm remedies and other medications, tooth cleaning, surgeries, grooming, dog walkers, and dog training are just the beginning. Then there are the myriad choices you have for items like designer canine furnishings, dog spas and resorts, special camps for dogs, dog accessories, treats from the dog bakery, color-coordinated clothing, holiday photos, and more. No wonder the profits for the pet industry have surpassed both the toy and the candy industry at $34 billion a year. According to an article in *USA Today*, you could spend $4,000 on a bed or $5,500 on a vest if you're so inclined. There was a time when folks didn't spend this kind of money on their pets, and there are still many people who don't. But there is so much available for dogs these days, that at some point, you will have to make decisions about all the choices.

Veterinary Care Mirrors Human Care

One of the biggest changes we've seen over the years in veterinary care is with the medical options vailable. There was a time when illness and severe medical conditions meant that your only choice was having to put down your dog. Now, the advances in surgery and medical care for canines allows for myriad choices. Dr. Russ Gurevitch, a northern California veterinary surgeon, shed understanding on the alternatives available to pooches and their parents. He said that the medical possibilities in today's society were not considered or anticipated when he was a young man entering veterinary school. Add to that the fact that dogs now serve functions they never did before. He says, "People's dogs are the nonjudgmental spouse that everyone wanted, or the child for those who never had kids, or even like an old parent that they push around in wheelchairs, buggies, or carts so they can get around. Given that we look at dogs more as members of the family, it isn't unreasonable to treat them that way, and there are more choices available. When I started my practice, I wasn't able to do the things

I can now. In the 'olden' days, a diagnosis would be made based on a guess. Now veterinarians have the ability to be very thorough in their diagnostics and come up with an exact treatment."

Dr. Gurevitch notes that virtually everything that's available in human medicine is now available in veterinary medicine: CAT scans, MRIs, laser, ultrasound, robotic surgery, arthroscopic surgery, laparoscopic surgery, bypass surgery, kidney transplants, joint replacement surgery, and cancer treatments. "Since most artificial organs were trialed in animals before being used in humans, they will be available in five to ten years for animals," he adds. "You'll be able to have a heart transplant, or some other organ for your dog."

An Invitation for Guilt

Now that all these choices are available, you'll have to make some very hard decisions when it comes to the care of your four-legged children. Will you be ready to plunk down between $10,000 and $30,000 for a medical procedure that might be the difference between life and death for your baby? Planning ahead can prevent guilt or help you deal with it. Herm and Rose decided to accept the "normal" life cycle of their chow chow, Millie's, life. They knew she would live approximately twelve years, and that they would feel very sad when she died. However, they decided in advance that they would not break their budget if Millie got a life threatening disease. Making the decision in advance eased any guilt they might have felt by having to agonize over a decision at the last minute.

Others decide to get pet insurance. When Lott and her husband became pooch parents, the thought of obtaining medical coverage for their dog seemed ludicrous to them. Today, given their experiences with their two dogs, they wouldn't hesitate to purchase such insurance if they were to start over. Veterinary pet insurance has been around since the late seventies and can radically cut your health care costs. Currently there are ten to twelve companies writing policies, as well as some veterinary practices that have their own clinic plan. If something goes wrong, insurance will save you a lot of money. For example, according to Dr. Gurevitch, the most common surgery is cruciate ligament repair (he does twenty a month), and the charge is $3,000 to $4,000. Pet insurance could cover a large chunk of that.

Insurance quotes are based on the age of your pooch and whether you want major medical, routine care, or both. As with humans, the longer you wait to get insurance, the more expensive it is and the more pre-existing conditions aren't covered. For more information, check out the Web for a list of insurance companies, or ask your veterinarian for recommendations. Given how difficult it is to leave something untreated that could be dealt with, and given how expensive veterinary care and surgery can be, we recommend taking out pet health insurance for your canine kid.

Is Having a Dog Worth the High Cost?

Dogs teach us many lessons about life, like how to enjoy a good walk, how to be a loyal friend, and how to show love. They provide warmth on a cold night, bark to keep away intruders, and are excellent listeners. Anyone who has loved a dog knows that whatever amount of money it takes to keep them, they more than earn their keep in the amount of comfort and love they provide.

"Owning a pet," according to a WebMD Feature in February 2004, "can ward off depression, lower blood pressure, and boost immunity. It may even improve your social life." The article went on to say that infants raised with dogs were less likely to show evidence of pet allergies and had signs of stronger immune systems. Dogs provide companionship for the elderly, improve the quality of life for patients diagnosed with terminal illnesses, and increase the survival rate for folks with heart attacks. In a study presented to the American Heart Association, people with pets experience half the increase in blood pressure when stressed.

Mayo Clinic cancer specialist Edward T. Creagan, MD, in an article in *Bottom Line*, included the following in his secret to living a long, healthy life: "Social connectedness, including the unconditional love of a pet, can protect against cancer. My wife and I have two golden retrievers—Brinkley and Jesse—and a cat named Reggie. [They]…give us the best medicine of all. I often write a 'pet prescription' for my patients."

If dogs could talk about the "money L," we're sure they'd say: "Stop your bellyaching. I'm worth every penny, and you know it!"

KIND AND FIRM PUP PARENTING PRINCIPLES

1. No matter how much you love your dog, don't forget to take care of practical matters.

2. Adjust your lifestyle to allow time for your dog's basic needs for love, time, and training.

3. Give up all notions of having a "House Beautiful" as you make changes in your living space to accommodate your dog. Focus on your love for your dog.

4. Thinking about your life phase means considering your dog's needs as well as your own.

5. Take time for training to acclimate your dog to inside living— where the best socialization training takes place.

6. Dogs need limits and boundaries. Choose the kind of confinement in your house that is respectful to the needs of you and your dog.

7. Borrow a dog for a week to experience what dog parenting is really like.

8. Don't kid yourself that most of the "things" you buy for your dog are really for him. Be honest and enjoy.

CHAPTER 4

DOG 101: WHAT EVERY PUP PARENT NEEDS TO KNOW

"That book we bought on dog-training? Howard is lying on it and won't get up."

—*Howard Huge cartoon*

We know a lot of folks whose dogs, like Howard, must have been lying on their training manuals. Could you be one of them? Ask yourself the following questions, and if the answers elude you, make sure you read the rest of this chapter. Though the information may seem clear-cut and obvious to some, we are constantly amazed at the number of pup parents who don't have answers to these questions. Often, this basic information is either unknown or ignored, and it results in disrespectful treatment to a dog, a neighbor, or you.

Where do I find the right dog for me?

Does my dog need daily walks?

Do I really need to pick up after my dog?

How long can I leave my dog home alone?

Do I need to fence my yard?
Is it really necessary to neuter or spay my pup?
What's the best way to transport my dog in the car?
Where should my dog sleep?
What do I do if my dog barks a lot?

We know you don't want to be a Dog 101 dropout, so please take this chapter very seriously. Even though you may have had dogs for years, you could still learn something new! And don't skip around, either, because we might just spring a pop quiz on you at the end of this chapter!

Finding the Right Dog for You

Even if you already have a dog, you'll find this information useful to help you better understand yourself and your dog. When we were kids (for some of us, a very long time ago), a lot of dogs came from a cardboard box in front of the grocery store. Today, most counties have laws against that because the dog that will spend the rest of his or her life with you should be genetically sound and healthy. "Backyard breeders" can't guarantee that.

A backyard breeder is a person who has a dog and thinks, "Wouldn't it be fun to see what the pups will look like," or "Wow, we could make some money selling puppies." This person has no experience breeding dogs or raising pups—not a good choice for you.

So how about buying a dog at the pet store? Most professionals would recommend against buying your dog from such a store because too often dogs are sold by breeders who care only about making money and not the health or quality of the dog. The price of a dog found in a pet store will most likely be highly inflated. While all that may be true, we're not ruling out pet stores completely. There are many pet stores that guarantee the dogs they sell and are extremely responsible in choosing where their dogs come from.

But how would you know if your pet store is responsible? Ask some questions about where the puppies came from, whether the dealer is licensed by the USDA, if the pups have genetic clearances, if copies of eye and hip certifications are available, and what happens to the pups they don't sell: Do they go to rescue groups, are they euthanized, or are they returned to the breeders? Most important, find out if the store will stand behind a dog that shows signs of genetic problems or becomes ill. You might even do your homework and check with the Better Business Bureau in your town to find out if there have been complaints against the store.

Since it is hard to walk away from an adorable pup (and what pup isn't adorable?) once you fall in love with him, do your research before you walk into the store. Any seller who is truly concerned about the welfare of the pups should be willing to answer your questions and possibly have some questions for you, too, to find out what kind of pup parent you're going to be.

Keep in mind that there are many pet stores that support "puppy mills," where dogs are kept for breeding purposes only and have more litters per year than is safe for the dog. The puppy mills don't treat either the bitch or the pups respectfully, and neglect prevails. In some cases, dogs aren't given the required shots, nor are the pups fed—often surviving by eating their own feces. The pups are often separated from their mother too early and don't get the training from her that helps them later. They aren't held or played with by humans, either. Dogs that have human contact early do much better with their socialization. To learn more about puppy mills, visit the Web site CanisMajor.com.

Since we've nixed the grocery store and the pet store, how about the want ads? We're sure that many of you have found the canine love of your life through the classifieds, but once again, buyer beware! If you are buying blind, you might save money, but you could end up with a dog that isn't healthy or right for you. You could be buying your dog from a backyard breeder or even a puppy mill. To help make a good choice, follow the guidelines we outlined for the pet store, and most important of all, make sure the seller is willing to stand behind the health of the dog. If the dog is a particular breed, the seller should know a lot about that breed and be willing and able to answer your questions about breed characteristics and special needs.

We hope that wherever you choose to get your animal, he or she comes with a health certificate from the breeder. When Lynn bought Magic, she wished she would have known to ask the breeder for a health certificate. The genetic testing that's available to breeders through the Orthopedic Foundation for Animals (OFA) would probably have picked up the congenital defect of blindness from cataracts. The OFA offers information "concerning orthopedic and genetic diseases of animals," and its goal is to "advise, encourage and establish control programs to lower the incidence of orthopedic and genetic diseases." By the time Lynn and Hal discovered that their Magic was blind, the breeder ignored all correspondence about the condition. Lynn was especially concerned that the breeder know of the condition so as to avoid future problems. If prospective pup parents insisted on seeing a health certificate before purchasing a puppy, the breeders might be more prone to correcting the problem.

As a savvy pup parent, be sure to ask the breeder whether this particular pup has been tested for hip or eye problems, two of the most common genetic defects. The OFA tests are reasonably priced for breeders, ranging from $15 to $30. Dogs with hip and eye problems can end up costing you thousands of dollars in veterinary bills. A responsible breeder wouldn't breed a dog that is known to have these problems.

Also make sure that the breeder has de-wormed and given all necessary shots to your pup. Ask the breeder for shot records to safeguard your dog's health. It's also a good idea to check whether the pup was raised inside with lots of time learning from its mother and littermates as well as loving human family members.

The Best Place to Find Your Pup

We recommend finding your dog from a reputable breeder or adopting a dog from your local SPCA, Humane Society, or Rescue Organization (see page 70). In addition to what we've already mentioned about finding a reputable breeder, make sure you have a conversation about the dog, the breeding conditions, and your parenting style. Some knowledgeable breeders will put you through the third degree, and that's great. They care about what happens to the puppies they sell. Some will insist that you sign an agreement of care spelling out what they expect from you as a pup parent. That's also good because this breeder is as interested in the future of the dog as in the money made from breeding. The breeder may want to know if you've had a dog before, where you live, whether you have children, and what your plans are for training and care.

Also, feel free to find out from the breeder whether you can visit the litter. (If you're really doing your homework—and you are, aren't you?—you might even visit that breeder's current or next litter before making your decision.) Keep in mind that you might spend a bundle traveling across the country to pick up your dog at a breeder's, and might make two trips to the breeder—one to see the new litter and select a puppy and one eight weeks later to pick up your baby. You could ask for names and phone numbers of other pup parents who have purchased dogs from that kennel; a reputable breeder should have no problem providing references like this. It is also important to know at what age the kennel places the pups into their new homes. A responsible breeder should never let a pup go before seven weeks of age—eight is preferable. If the breeder wants to get rid of a dog sooner, find a different breeder.

If you're looking for a particular breed—and you probably have your reasons—we hope that you've taken the time to spend with adult dogs from that breed before getting a puppy or even adopting a rescue. If you don't know, ask the breeder to tell you about the pros and the cons of the breed. They should know both and be happy to share the information with you. You can also ask whether the breeder will let you talk to his veterinarian to learn more about the health history and how much genetic testing has been done on the dam and sire. Don't forget that all-important question about the breeder's return policy if there are health problems.

If the breeder has too many different breeds, or a huge number of dogs, take caution. The puppies may not be well socialized by their parents. Lynn bought her miniature schnauzer, Magic, from such a kennel, and if she had been aware of this information, it might have influenced her decision in another direction. There were many signs that the breeder wasn't a good choice, including the fact that there were pups from four or five different breeds in the dog yard. But Lynn had spent time with another mini from this kennel who was a wonderful adult dog, and that swayed her opinion.

Lynn would be the first to say that Magic is an exceptional dog, regardless of the genetic problems she came home with, and that she has never regretted having Magic in the family, in spite of her many health issues. But she and Hal have spent thousands of dollars on these problems, and they suggest you do your homework if you'd like to avoid the emotional and financial strain that comes from having a dog with serious health problems.

If you think that spending more money or getting an AKC-registered dog will ensure a problem-free pup, think again. According to information found on the American Kennel Club Web site, "There is a widely held belief that 'AKC' or 'AKC papers' guarantee the quality of a dog. This is not the case. AKC is a registry body and breed registrations don't include site visits to the kennels. A registration certificate identifies the dog as the offspring of a known sire and dam, born on a known date. It in no way indicates the quality or state of health of the dog." Know that a dog that runs over $1,000 can still have genetic problems.

Like Lynn and Hal, Connie and Chance decided to keep their pup, even after problems developed. They searched long and hard for the dog of their dreams—a miniature Australian shepherd—asking a lot of questions and doing a lot of research. They brought their puppy, Gretchen, home on a Saturday evening. It was her first night away from her dog mommy, a thought that devastated Connie to the point that it was hard to tell who was sadder: Connie or Gretchen. At one point, Gretchen was so upset, she howled at the moon. She got diarrhea and kept everyone up all night. Since she was only seven pounds to start with, Connie and Chance decided to take her to the vet to make sure she wasn't dehydrated. The vet discovered that, although she wasn't dehydrated, she did have a heart murmur. Further conversation revealed that she would either die from the heart murmur or grow out of it.

Connie and Chance were distraught, and all the advice from well-meaning friends to return her because she was "faulty" didn't help. When they spoke with the breeder, she assured them that they could bring the dog back and pick another pup from the litter. Even though they had only spent one night with Gretchen, she was already their baby—their first baby, and they had no intention of returning her. That's how quickly they bonded with their dog. Fortunately, Gretchen outgrew the heart murmur and has become the family "love bug."

> If dogs could talk, we think they might say, "It's hard enough leaving our mom and siblings behind. Thanks for making sure we're the right dog for you so we don't have to go through that separation again."

Adopting a Dog Has Many Rewards

There's another choice for finding your dog: adoption. Adopted dogs are usually nine months or older, so you get to skip the time, energy, and work of the early puppy stage. (Of course, many believe the puppy stage is half the joy of parenting a dog and are willing to pay the time and energy price.) Some folks think that adopting a dog is adopting someone else's problems. Sometimes that is the case, but not always. While some of the dogs at the public shelter could be there because they bark too much, chew the furniture, bite, roam, or have health problems, others may have problems because no one took the time to train them or give them the attention they needed. When you get a dog from the shelter, you are often getting a dog without a known history (or one that might be slightly skewed), and that can be difficult for folks who aren't ready for surprises. If you think the dog from the shelter will love and appreciate you because you saved it from death or loneliness, and that that same dog will behave perfectly to show her gratitude, you are living in a world of make-believe.

Bart's history wasn't so unusual for a dog needing rescue. His first family left town and gave him to a friend. The friend left Bart alone for hours at a time in a small bedroom. Bart entertained himself by chewing a hole through the wall, at which point his new family gave him up for adoption. His next family, the Sharps, said that Bart was a great dog—as long as he was with the family. But if they left him alone for a few hours, he became anxious and agitated. After a few years, he was so agitated that he couldn't or wouldn't sleep. He started a downhill decline, and despite their best efforts at training and medication, Bart eventually had to be euthanized.

Fortunately, most adopted dogs don't follow Bart's fate. We have heard countless success stories from pup parents who found their dog at the shelter, gave her the attention and love she needed, and have shared years of joy together. That was the case with Snickers, a German shepherd, whom the Sharps adopted next. Snickers came well trained from his stint in the Seeing Eye training program. There's a long list of people waiting to get a dog that doesn't complete the training, so it can be a long wait for one of their dogs. The Sharps, however, felt it was worth it to hold out for a well-trained dog who would be gentle and who wouldn't chew holes in the walls.

In addition to public shelters, there are also many private shelters where you can find a dog; often they are noneuthanizing facilities. One of the most elaborate shelters, the Animal Rescue Foundation, was founded by Tony La Russa, San Francisco Bay Area baseball man, and his wife, Elaine, to help animal orphans and to encourage people to adopt dogs. Complete with conference rooms, educational facilities, and clinics for spaying and neutering, ARF is a 37,700-square-foot center that the La Russas, as reported in the *San Francisco Chronicle*, hope will become as famous as other Bay Area attractions, like the cable cars or Alcatraz.

As we have said, do not assume that the dog in the shelter or from the rescue group is a problem dog. Many dogs end up in a shelter because someone developed an allergy, or having a dog became more work and time than the pup parent bargained for. Maybe someone died, became ill, got divorced, moved, or got a new job that requires a lot of travel and could no longer care for their dog. When you get a dog from a shelter or from a rescue group, it will have been spayed or neutered (or will have to be before it leaves), probably house-trained because it is an older dog, have had the necessary shots, and will most often respond positively to your good parenting efforts. Perhaps the dog is even obedience-trained, or training is part of the package provided by the shelter.

We hope you will seriously consider exploring adoption when choosing the right dog for your family. Like any wise adoptive parent, ask a lot of questions as to the behavior, history, and health of the animal, including vaccinations. Visit the shelter and see how the staff interacts with the animals and keeps the place. Also ask about training referrals and the return policy.

If dogs could talk, we think they might say: "Bet you didn't realize how complicated it could be to find a healthy pup. We're counting on you to do your homework so our future brothers and sisters are treated right by their breeders."

Your Dog Needs Daily Walks

After you've chosen the dog for your family and you've set up your home, you'll also need to set up routines that accommodate having a dog in the house. One of the most important habits you can start right now is to make time to take your dog for walks. Dogs love to walk with you. If you're going to be a responsible pup parent, find a way to fit in at least one walk a day. The easiest way is to create a schedule for yourself that is realistic—is walking during your morning rush to leave the house even feasible, or will a walk fit in better as part of your after-work downtime?—and then stick to your routine. Your dog will be waiting for that walk just like little kids wait for snack time at preschool or how some people wait for that cocktail before dinner.

Schedules that are linked to your normal routines usually work best. If you always eat dinner at 6:00, plan to walk your dog at 5:30, just before dinner. Or walk your dog right after dinner. It's both great for your dog and good for your digestion. If you always go to bed at 10:00, consider walking your dog at 9:30. If you're an early riser, walk your dog after you read the morning paper and have your first cup of coffee. By making that walk one of *your* routines, your dog will help you keep it, often waiting by the door or running at the sound of the leash coming off the hook.

How far you walk is up to you and your dog, but we're sure that you won't find better quality time with your pup. You may consider a walk around the block long enough, or a short jaunt to your mailbox, or to the corner. It's still a walk, although we hope that once you get out there with your dog and start walking, you'll walk a bit further than a block. Keep in mind that a dog that gets used to walking three miles a day has no problem with that distance—until she gets older and can't keep up anymore. Your dog will let you know when that happens. Some dogs will jog with you or hike with you, running as many miles as you do, or more. When you choose a dog, think about how you want the dog to fit into your lifestyle and then research to find out if the breed can handle your expectations.

You probably wouldn't take your English bulldog on your five-mile daily run, would you?

The chart on pages 76–77 gives general information about types of breeds and their common characteristics. We realize there are exceptions to every rule, but if you want a dog who loves to run, you might want to avoid the toy group. If you're looking for a dog who will hike with you without running away, you're taking a big chance with sporting dogs and working dogs. Likewise, if you see yourself taking short strolls and spending a lot of time with your dog in your lap, a hound wouldn't be a good choice.

It's best not to walk your dog (or yourself) at the hottest time of day, unless you have plenty of water. Even then, choosing a cooler time of day would be better for all. When you take your dog for a walk, whether you are walking on a city sidewalk, park trail, or playing in a dog yard, make sure she's on a leash. If you are wondering when you can take your dog off-leash, we suggest you consider the following: your dog's temperament and personality, your location, and the level of your voice control. If your dog has any aggression problems directed at either dogs or people, off-leash in public places is out of the question for obvious reasons. Other factors are your dog's predatory and chase drives, such as a dog that will chase anything that moves fast: people on bicycles, skateboards, running children, etc.

Does your dog's social drive override his willingness to respond to you? Some dogs, regardless of breed, can't resist saying hello to every other dog on the way. Others will hide between your legs, refusing to acknowledge that another dog is nearby. Again, refer to the chart on pages 76–77 as well as your own relationship with your dog to help you understand her better. Lynn's Magic won't cross a border into a dog park until her parents snap on her leash. Strange behavior, but true. Follow your dog's lead and you'll discover what degree of sociability she has.

Location includes proximity to traffic; events such as a ball game in progress or picnicking people; terrain problems, and wildlife. Obviously, you need to keep your dog on a leash if traffic and/or people at play are present. For many dogs, you'll be glad you use the leash if the area is filled with foxtails, weeds, ticks, and/or dangerous snakes. It is imperative that you respect laws that prohibit dogs in areas where there are nesting mammals and birds. They have the right to be there without being terrorized and harassed by a frolicking canine. These places are usually state or national parks or wildlife habitats, which are not places to turn your dog loose.

Neither should your dog be off-leash if he won't come to you when instructed to do so—either when you use a whistle and/or a recall command. If you want your high-energy dog to be able to run freely, a 60- to 70-foot line (⅛-inch parachute cord) can be safely used in any large open space—one without obstacles or tall grass or weeds—when it's not practical and safe for your dog to be off-leash. Be sure to wear gloves while working with a long line so you don't end up with rope burns. Hold one end in your hand and attach the other end to your dog's collar. Then pick up the slack in the line and walk the line through your hands as your dog moves farther away and closer to you.

With the long line, your dog has complete freedom—and you have complete control at your fingertips. You can practice your recalls (see Chapter 6 for instructions) since you have a way to enforce them without getting into trouble. Ball and Frisbee work can also be done nicely on a long line. This line, as opposed to allowing your dog off-leash, is the only option for a dog that has aggressive tendencies. You'll need to find a place that is unoccupied to exercise your dog. Keep your dog on the long line, and if you see another dog or person coming, reel your dog in—fast. For a dog that is a runner, a dog for whom freedom is a top priority and for whom coming to you for a food reward or a ball is a low priority, the long line is perfect. Your dog has room to play and explore, but will come to you because he or she is still attached and you have some control.

Many areas have dog parks where you can safely take your dog off-leash so he or she can frolic freely and socialize with other dogs. (Do not bring an aggressive dog to a dog park for obvious reasons.) Some people substitute the retractable leash for the long line. It doesn't have as much length, but it can allow your dog a

(continued on page 78)

DOG GROUPS AND BREEDS

Dog Group	Original Purpose	Unique Traits	Special Needs	Representative Breeds
Sporting	To search for and retrieve birds and small mammals	Enthusiastic, active, and alert, strong desire to please, focused, nonterritorial, not dominant, keen sense of smell, soft mouth	Fencing or confinement as they will follow their nose, vigorous exercise, field work	Pointers, retrievers, spaniels, setters
Herding Group	Control the movement of other animals	Protective, independent thinking, strong chase instinct, very territorial, can be quite content with indoor life and they bond closely with their human family	Socialization, lots of human contact, will not be mindlessly obedient, but respond well to training	Australian shepherd, Bouvier des Flandres, collie, corgi, rottweiler, shepherd
Working Group	To assist in activities requiring strength and or endurance—guarding property, pulling sleds, water rescue	Alert, courageous, hardy, territorial, and protective	To have work to do, by virtue of their size and strength, they must be trained	Akita, Doberman pinscher, Great Dane, husky, malamute, St. Bernard, Samoyed, water dogs
Non-Sporting Group	Various instincts and characteristics—very diversified group	Companion animals	Socialization, lots of human contact	Bulldog, chow chow, dalmatian, Lhasa apso, poodle

Dog Group	Original Purpose	Unique Traits	Special Needs	Representative Breeds
Hound Group	Use sense of sight and smell to help hunters track game	Pleasant personalities, very "pack" sociable, more independent than sporting dogs and will range farther afield while hunting, nonterritorial, have a distinctive "baying" sound	Because of their strong chase instinct, they must be confined, need vigorous exercise and the opportunity to follow their instincts	Afghan hound, basset hound, beagle, bloodhound, dachshund, greyhound, Rhodesian ridgeback, whippet
Terrier Group	To hunt and kill vermin	Sturdy and fearless, feisty and confident, curious and dominant, playful and outgoing with people, but not always good around other dogs, a lot of bark	Need strong training, as many retain a strong prey instinct and will fight for dominance in the family, many require special grooming technique called "stripping"	Airedale, border terrier, cairn terrier, Jack Russell terrier, miniature schnauzer, pit bull terrier
Toy Group	Companionship and entertainment	Usually mild-mannered and with sweet tempera-ments, portable!	Human interaction	Cavalier King Charles spaniel, Chihuahua, Maltese, Pekingese, Pomeranian, shih tzu, toy poodle

certain amount of exploration room while still being safely close by and within your control.

It helps to know your dog when making a final decision about leash or no leash. Britt, a spayed female Lab, and Beowolf, an intact male Akita, are two dogs owned by two different women. Britt is a stereotypical female Lab, if there is such a thing. She wouldn't dream of not staying close to Mom or coming when called. She also has very high food drives. Her mom can take her off-leash in any public place, providing it is safe for Britt. Beowolf, on the other hand, has a different agenda altogether. Being a ring tail (Nordic and Far East breed with a tail that curves over the back of the dog), he is highly independent, and recalls are low on his list of priorities. He's likely to drift away, follow a scent, and completely tune out his parent. He's also very inclined to play catch-me games. Most Nordic and Far East breeds like this annoying game, which makes owners feel desperate and look incompetent. We wouldn't recommend that his mom take Beowolf off-leash in an unfenced area.

> If dogs could talk, we think they might say: "We know you think we need a lot of freedom, but we can get into more trouble than you ever imagined, so keep us on a leash, please."

Cleaning Up after Your Dog Isn't a Courtesy—It's a Must

This one seems like a no-brainer, but maybe you've seen the billboards announcing, SAVE OUR WATERWAYS. CLEAN UP AFTER ME, with a picture of a dog on it. That's because many pup parents think dog poop is biodegradable like the droppings from horses, cows, deer, or rabbits, who are all vegetarians. But quite to the contrary, dog feces stay on the ground for a long time, attract flies, and can spread viral disease and parasites, not to mention the unpleasantness for other people using a public area—or the as equal unpleasantness if your own backyard becomes too…crowded.

We once saw a father pushing twins in a stroller and walking a dog on a leash in a public park. When the dog stepped off the trail to "do his business," Dad said, "Whose turn is it to pick up after the dog?" One of the children grabbed a bag, picked up the poop, and handed it to Dad, who put it in the trash receptacle. The child couldn't have been much older than three, but was happy to be Daddy's helper—a future savvy pup parent in the making.

Save your bags from the grocery store or from your home-delivered newspaper and recycle them when cleaning up after your dog. Many dog parks even supply doggy bags in handy containers. Use them. If you're not a user of plastic bags, a quick online search will send you to hundreds of sites that sell bags specifically for doggies; your local pet store also sells them, along with a leash that has a little pouch to keep them in.

For all the reasons we've already mentioned, you also need to clean up after your dog in your backyard or wherever you let your dog play when you aren't around. One of the easiest pieces of equipment is a long-handled rake and long-handled dustpan set. You don't even have to bend over to clean the yard during "poo patrol." One family pays their children by the "poop pile" to do yard clean up. An enterprising eight-year-old could make enough money from a normal dog to buy something special in no time flat!

Leaving Dogs Home Alone

Dogs left alone for long periods of time are being asked to conform to something for which they are not genetically programmed. This lifestyle is very unnatural for animals with social and exercise needs. Isolation from the rest of the family on a regular basis often leads to destructiveness, escape behavior, nuisance barking, and behaviors that may be related to separation anxiety. A large number of behavior and training problems are directly related to how many hours the dog spends at home alone. A dog left inside all day can destroy property, become depressed, soil carpets, or bark incessantly. Even the dog who spends many hours alone outside will have a lot of pent-up energy—and makes it a daily activity to create exercise and entertainment for himself by running around the yard, digging, and barking at everything he sees. If your dog is doing any of these behaviors, consider them signs that it is time to make some changes in the amount of time your dog spends alone.

Even if you've followed all the suggestions for dog-proofing your living space (including crating), as found in Chapter 3, you'll still need to figure out how to make sure your dog knows she is part of your family when she's left alone. Though there isn't an exact-hour amount of time that is too long to leave a dog, some can handle being home alone for up to ten hours, while many can't handle alone time for more than four or five.

Some parents solve the problem of too much alone time by taking their dog to work, as did Carol, a prominent family law attorney with a very successful mediation practice. She decided to bring her little dog, Happy, a West Highland terrier, to work with her every day. Happy sat quietly in his special, comfy chair and was very well behaved. He didn't bark, he didn't jump on the clients, and he didn't interrupt Carol. His time at home was a different matter. He barked incessantly, jumped on everyone who came into the house, and ran around yipping wildly. When Carol was asked why he behaved so well at work, she laughed and said, "Because I expect it! And because I follow through. At home, I get lazy and use a lot of words, threats, and no follow-through."

Verbalizing that was an ah-ha for Carol. She realized that Happy was perfectly able to behave himself at work, so perhaps, if she talked less and followed through more, he could do the same at home. When she changed her ways, Happy followed suit and improved his behavior. Perhaps if Carol had never taken her dog to work she would not have realized how easy he was to train. And if Carol had left her dog at home for long periods of time, perhaps he would have become one of those dogs who bark incessantly.

Other pup parents drop their dogs off at doggy day care (more about that in Chapter 9). Hiring a dog walker who will come in during the day and play with or walk your dog is another possibility.

Maria, mother to a six-year-old toy poodle, Theadora (Teddi for short), solves the problem by taking her dog for an hour-long walk every morning before she goes to work and then playing ball and hide-and-seek for an hour when she gets home. You might think that an hour is too long for such a small dog, but if you met this toy poodle, you'd realize how lucky Maria is to get off so easily, as her dog would walk for two hours if Maria would let her.

In another family, Blair swears that his dachshund, Greta, doesn't mind his being at work because he leaves the sliding door on their enclosed, elevated deck open wide enough for her to go in and out at will. He also leaves the television on to Animal Planet, so his dog can "watch TV" instead of facing boredom. We're not convinced that watching television is necessary for Greta, but it certainly doesn't hurt, and Blair also spends a lot of quality time with her when he does get home, which is likely why Greta is so well behaved.

Another dog parent, Janelle, combined many of the solutions we've mentioned so that she could feel secure that her new German shepherd pup, Frankie, would be able to handle spending time alone while she worked a 40-hour week. Her efforts were focused on creating quality time for her dog, knowing that quality was more important than quantity. She substituted her guilt about her lifestyle with positive actions.

Janelle knew that German shepherds can have serious issues being left home alone, as they are bred to live and work closely with people and are highly social in nature. Also, they are highly intelligent and need mental stimulation. They are happiest when they are busy doing some activity—not by themselves, but as a team with their parent or family. Knowing this, Janelle included Frankie in almost all of her social activities. Frankie began learning right from the start how to fit in and share Janelle's life. On weekends they went camping and hiking together, and several evenings a week, she brought Frankie with her to the homes of her friends, where she got to visit and socialize with people as well as other dogs. She took Frankie for a long walk almost every day after work, went to one of the local dog parks as often as she could, and also invited friends over to her home frequently. If Janelle had to stay late at work, she arranged for a pet sitter/pet walker to come to her home and spend time with Frankie and take her for a walk.

Frankie, a sweet, friendly dog to begin with, matured into a very well-behaved and highly socialized dog who felt secure and confident with her lifestyle. Due to the fact that Janelle was willing to include Frankie to such a large extent in her life, Frankie never became anxious and destructive when Janelle was at work. Janelle gave Frankie a specially baited marrow bone just before she left to make her departure as positive an experience as possible.

> If dogs could talk, we think they might say: "We understand that sometimes you have to go it alone, but we love being included in the family any chance you have to take us with you to meet your friends."

A Fenced-In Dog Is a Happy Dog

Most dogs enjoy a certain amount of time outside, whether playing, exploring, or watching the world go by. Allowing a dog to play in the yard alone is quite different from banishing your dog to the yard. Most parents will let their children spend time outside once they know they are safe. The same is true for your dog once you've made adjustments for both safety and good-neighborliness. Since there is no boundary training that is 100 percent reliable, we suggest you have a fenced-in yard.

If you're thinking, "But *my* dog stays within her boundaries *most of the time*," we'd like to point out that it takes only once for a car to injure or kill your dog. How many dogs can resist the temptation of a cat on the other side of the street, or a squirrel, another dog, or a child? Do you really want your dog wandering freely throughout the neighborhood, knocking over little kids, causing or being involved in traffic accidents, getting inadvertently poisoned, or defecating on other people's lawns? We hope not. You can prevent World War III in your neighborhood, or painful losses to you or your pooch, by using one of our recommended fencing options.

The most obvious fencing option is to find an area for your dog and fence it in with wood, wire, mesh, or any material that is both safe and fits in with your setting. Some families create dog runs or fence in an entire yard. But there are times when traditional fencing isn't possible due to terrain, size of your lot, or neighborhood rules. In these cases, you might consider an invisible or hidden fence system. This is a wire that can either be buried underground or stretched along an already existing fence, and is then hooked up to a transmitter in the garage. It works by signaling to a small receiver on the dog's collar, which gives him an audio warning if he enters a field that is pre-set; if he ignores this warning, he will receive a very, very mild electrical stimulation in the collar. The fence allows you to block off any size area you choose, while at the same time excluding parts of the area where you don't want the dog such as landscaped areas, swimming pools, etc. Your house and driveway should be included in the field of the system so the dog can go in and out of the house and in and out of the car without having to cross the wire. Many dogs have enormous respect for the fence line after one correction.

For some dogs, there can be serious problems resulting from improper installation or improper training once an invisible fence system is established. If you have a breed that is prone to aggression problems, you are taking a big chance combining electricity with your dog. That's why we recommend finding a dealer who will come to your property to help you install the fence and then train you and your dog. An improperly installed invisible fence could result in changes to your dog's disposition, which could lead to your dog being sent to a shelter.

If neither traditional nor invisible fencing will work for you, there are other systems to consider. One containment possibility is called the trolley system. It consists of a run line made of aircraft cable (check Loosco.com or Pet-Collars.com for more information) that runs between two high points, such as two trees or the corner of the house and a tree. A trolley with a ten-foot down cable for the dog allows the dog more mobility than a cable that is attached to a stationary object. It's safer because of the angle of the cable so it doesn't tangle, providing there is no other obstacle in the way between the two points where the run line is attached. There may be times when this is the only solution, especially if dealing with an escape artist (a jumper and/or a digger). The down cable must be attached to a buckle collar and *never* to a choke collar.

The best use of the trolley system would be when your dog is left on the run line for short periods while you are on the property. If your dog is alone and unsupervised for a majority of the day, the system has many drawbacks, especially if your pooch is vulnerable to attacks from other animals. Great care must be taken that there is adequate shelter when using the trolley system.

Notice that we don't recommend tying a dog up with a short chain or rope, even though it's a solution that seems so simple and inexpensive. This practice deprives your dog of most of his social needs, not to mention that shelter in such cases is completely inadequate. Dogs that are tied up in such fashion (even when you use a swivel chain) almost always end up suffering when their water is knocked over, their line gets tangled in shrubs and hoses, and shade is impossible to find.

Putting your dog on a short chain can lead to frustration and induced aggression, which can result in unnecessary biting incidents. The dog is also vulnerable to misguided individuals who often think it's fun and exciting to tease him. This often happens in the absence of the owners, who usually have no idea this is occurring while they are gone. That was the case with a St. Bernard who escaped and terrorized Jane's son Kenny when he was only nine years old. They lived near a St. Bernard who had developed a mean disposition because he was always tied to a short chain. Kids would tease him and make him bark—as long as they felt safe because he was chained. One day the St. Bernard got loose from his chain and started to bark and chase Kenny, who ran into a canyon to escape the dog. Every time he tried to get back to the street he would hear barking dogs, get scared, and run back and hide. Kenny ended up spending the whole night in a dry riverbed only a few miles from his home because he was afraid the dog would find him. No responsible pup parent would want their dog scaring a child the way this St. Bernard did.

If you do leave your dog in the yard when you are gone, in addition to using the proper fencing, you'll also need to provide shelter. Make sure you have a covered (and if necessary, warm) area for your dog. Garage access, if possible, works well. If you don't want your dog running freely inside the garage, you could construct a small fenced-in area just inside the door or set up an ex-pen if you have a small dog. Or your dog could have access to a porch, utility room, or some other enclosed area.

If you decide to use a doghouse for shelter, make sure it has a protected entrance so that your dog stays warm and dry once inside. A hinged roof makes cleaning easier, and elevating the doghouse a few inches on concrete piers keeps it warmer and dryer. Straw is superior for bedding, as it can't be pulled out by your dog and left in the elements like a rug or a blanket can.

> If dogs could talk, we think they might say: "You think that fence is there to keep us in, but we like the fence to keep out the troublemakers."

Spaying and/or Neutering Is Good for Your Dog

In 2004, it cost about $60 to spay a female and $130 to neuter a male—small costs compared to the problems you can have when you don't make this responsible choice. Are you aware of the part hormones play on your dog's overall behavior and the ability to learn and retain commands? Several weeks before a female comes in season and during the season, she displays erratic behavior that makes learning very difficult. An intact male is "in heat" 365 days a year and is focused primarily on scents in the air and on the ground, so his responsiveness to training is greatly diminished. These are great motivations for spaying and neutering. Testosterone usually adds fuel to an already existing problem. Though neutering isn't a cure-all, it's a place to start to get to the bottom of a dog's behavioral problems so that you aren't working against yourself while trying to stop bad behavior in your pet.

Testosterone doesn't affect all male dogs the same way. It depends a lot on the breed and individual personality. There won't be the same ramifications with an intact male poodle or sheltie as there would be with an intact male rottweiler or Akita. Rottweilers and Akitas are protection breeds that may have inherent potential aggression and dominant personalities. Regardless of breed and heritage, hormones can make a male dog restless and anxious, and the ever-present drive to roam and follow his nose is very strong. Any male dog will become a more trainable, responsive, happy, and calm family member when neutered.

Male aggression toward other male dogs can often become a huge problem. An intact dog—even if his disposition makes him generally not interested in picking fights with other dogs—will still emit a testosterone scent, which will attract other intact males who may see him as a threat or rival. The other dog may attack, try to pick a fight, or assert dominance. Sometimes the most subordinate dog can learn to fight because of a need to defend himself, and you could end up with a dog who becomes a fighter.

There are also medical reasons for spaying and neutering, including prostate and testicular cancer in males, and, in females, mammary gland tumors (breast cancer) and pyometra, an often fatal infection of the uterus. The incidents of these potential problems can be eliminated or greatly reduced with spaying and neutering.

Although it is best to spay or neuter your dog before it's six months old to avoid unwanted and unneeded pregnancies, this practice can be done at any age. Recent research has shown that dogs can be safely sterilized as early as eight weeks with few or no known side effects. Animal shelters all over the country are now practicing early sterilization in an attempt to curb the ever-increasing problem of over-population. Responsible breeders are taking advantage of early sterilization as a way to ensure that puppies they sell as pets will never be bred.

Neutering before six months is necessary to achieve maximum results. Although it is never too late, neutering a male after sexual maturity is not as effective because the behavior patterns related to hormone development have already had a chance to establish themselves. Though a lot of aggression toward owners and other people is not hormone related, a dog that is already genetically programmed to be dominant can often become much more dominant and aggressive if left intact because his hormones are feeding his desire to be bossy.

Some canine parents are against spaying and neutering their dogs, even after they find out that many of the problems they are trying to cope with, especially with their male dogs, are directly related to hormonal influences on their dog's behavior. These parents want to let their female dog have "just one litter" to see how cute the puppies will be and to allow the dog to be fulfilled. Not only does your female not need puppies to feel fulfilled; the world doesn't need more dogs that may end up in a shelter.

*If dogs could talk, we think they might say: "Watch out for that projection stuff. We know **you** like being parents, but **we're** quite happy not giving birth to doggy children."*

Transporting Dogs in the Car

You may have a lifestyle that involves hours in your car, and you like your dog to go with you. If that's the case, we hope you won't be like Deanna. She loved her little shih tzu, Scarlet, so much that she did everything she could to help Scarlet feel secure, including endangering herself and her dog by allowing Scarlet to sit on her shoulders while she was driving. Scarlet would fall asleep and slide down Deanna's back so she had to hunch over while driving—a very uncomfortable and dangerous position. Deanna's daughter, Kim, who also loved Scarlet very much, cured her of her shoulder-sitting habit. "I just wouldn't let her sit on my shoulders," she said.

This reflects a profound training method—your kind and firm expectations and follow-through.

Many people have developed the habit of letting their dog ride in the passenger seat next to them. This is a mistake, mainly for safety reasons. If you have a fairly large dog, your view can be obstructed. If you encounter an emergency and need to brake suddenly, your dog could get injured by hitting the windshield or by the air bag. If you have to make a sharp turn, your dog could end up bumping into or falling over you.

Your dog is safest in the back seat. Use either a special harness for your dog that hooks on to a seat belt, a doggy car seat that elevates your dog so he or she can watch out the window, or a leash that attaches to the seat belt. All of these items can be found at a pet store or on the Internet. If your car is a station wagon or sport-utility vehicle, the best way to transport your dog is in the far back of the car using a crate or a grill to create a safe, convenient compartment for the dog. This is how Lynn's dogs ride in the car, and they love going everywhere with the family, no matter how long the trip. They're so quiet, it's easy to forget they're back there. All it takes to get them ready is to ask, "Would you like to go to the movies?" Or, "Should we go to the bakery?" Or, "Anyone want to go to Tahoe?" and both dogs are standing with noses to the door, ready for an adventure.

If you have a pickup truck without a camper shell, you have only two options: in the cab with you with the leash attached either to the door handle or some other device that keeps your dog from reaching you, or a crate in the pickup bed securely fastened with bungee cords or something similar that will prevent it from tipping over or sliding. Unfortunately, it is common practice for some people to keep dogs in the back of a pickup either loose, which is illegal in some communities and a totally unacceptable option for safety reasons, or to use a commercially available device that allows the dog to be secured in the pickup bed without being able to reach the sides. If you have an accident, the device could break and your dog could tumble out of the truck to certain death or severe injury, not to mention the serious hazard to traffic. Also, keeping a dog in the pickup bed can be very damaging to the dog's eyes with debris flying through the air. In hot weather, unless you have carpeting in your pickup, the metal will heat up to an unacceptable degree and hurt the dog's feet. It's an excellent idea to transport a dog in a pickup with a camper shell with adequate flooring (not the metal bed itself) and with windows on the side for ventilation, or a window between the cab and the camper shell, so the dog can feel close to you.

Start training your dogs early if you want them to get used to traveling in a car with you. Use one of our recommended forms of containment or a crate. Leave a bowl of water in the car, along with some type of animal product such as a baited bone or a hoof. And lock your doors; if your dog is well socialized, valuable, and friendly, he could become a dog-napping victim. In hot or even warm weather you must *never* leave your dog in the car, even in the shade. Even with windows cracked open and in the shade, the temperature inside the car can be fifteen to twenty degrees hotter than outside, and your dog can die of hyperthermia.

> If dogs could talk, we think they might say: "Riding in the car is almost as much fun as going for walks with you. Thanks for taking me along and keeping me safe."

The Dog's Sleeping Arrangements

Does your dog need to sleep in the bedroom with you? Perhaps. But does your dog need to end up in your bed? Absolutely not. Does your dog often end up in bed with you anyway? More times than you'd like, we'll bet. Is your dog in bed with you by choice—yours or the dog's? We've heard that six out of ten dogs share their people's beds, and we'd guess that most of those dogs are in that bed because it's what they want more than what their pup parents want. Otherwise, why would we hear so many complaints about dogs keeping folks up all night with their snoring, or sleeping crosswise on the bed, or refusing to let their parents cuddle, getting in between, or even snarling if either person tries to initiate contact? Are you really willing to give up your sex life for your dog? Then there are those dog hairs and fleas and dirt, or the dog that won't move from the end of the bed and there's no room for your feet. The worst-case scenario is a dog that won't allow your partner or children to climb in bed with you while he's there. This behavior is totally unacceptable.

If you'd like your dog to sleep in the bedroom but not in your bed, you might want to review pages 32–34 in Chapter 2, where Bette and Bob used the Pup Parenting Plan to keep Buster out of their bed. So that you don't create the problems they did, we suggest you start when your pup is young. Don't let her get into the habit of sharing your pillow! Get your dog a crate, a dog bed, a pillow, or a rug, and when your dog tries to climb up on your bed, simply say, "Go to your bed." Then, if your dog doesn't move, stop using words and take action. Kindly and firmly remove your dog from your bed and place her on her bed. If you do this repeatedly, without emotion, your dog will figure out where her bed really is. If this doesn't work, get a crate for your dog to sleep in. At first, you'll need to close the door to the crate. Eventually, she will learn to stay in the crate even when the door is open.

If your dog cries at night, we recommend sitting on the floor next to her and petting her using gentle words like, "There, there, there." Even singing or humming can work, unless of course, your dog starts howling along! Then go back to "There, there, there." You may have to do this a few times, but usually this reassurance will help. As your dog gets a little older, the crying usually goes away.

It won't confuse your dog to have special times in bed with you to cuddle and play. Your dog will know the difference between sleeping in your bed and having short cuddle times—based on your attitude and your kindness and firmness regarding your expectations.

If dogs could talk, we think they might say: "Haven't you noticed that during the day we can sleep anywhere?"

If Your Dog Barks a Lot...

A barking dog is not a problem in and of itself. It only becomes a problem when people living nearby start complaining. That's when you have to take action because it can either lead to an abatement order from some authority (endangering your dog's life), or poor relations with your neighbors.

Dogs bark for a variety of reasons: boredom, isolation, stimuli surrounding the yard, fear and anxiety, barrier frustration, and for territorial reasons. It's helpful to do some fact-finding to pinpoint the reason (and to be sure that it *is* your dog doing the barking) and to formulate a plan based on your conclusions. We've discussed at length in this chapter how to prevent boredom, isolation, external stimuli, and barrier frustration. If you are dealing with complaints from neighbors, we suggest you take them very seriously. Start by asking for help from a friendly neighbor or using a voice-activated tape recorder to make sure the barking is coming from your dog. If your dog is the problem, take action immediately, before an irate neighbor decides to take matters into his or her own hands. We've heard of incidents of poisoning, and we wouldn't want that to happen to your dog.

A dog behaviorist may be able to help you with this problem. Dogs respond to noise stimulus, so you might be able to retrain your dog to stop barking by hiding on the other side of the fence, waiting till the dog barked, then throwing a chain at the fence or rattling a can filled with pebbles to make noise. Within a few days, the dog may well have stopped barking. If that doesn't work for you, you could also leave your dog at a friend's house, use doggy day care, hire a dog walker, take your dog to work with you, or worst case, find a different home for your dog. We've found that regularly running (not walking) your dog and obedience training often solve the problem.

Even dogs who remain indoors can cause a lot of neighborly discord, especially if you live in an apartment. If that's the case with your dog, in addition to what we've already suggested, try the following. If your dog has access to a window and barks at movement outside, keep him in a windowless room, or a room where the windows are too high for him to see out of. If he barks when someone rings the bell or knocks, praise your dog for letting you know that someone is approaching the house. You could do this verbally or with a treat. Then, if the barking persists, say in a calm and firm voice, "Ah, ah!" holding out your hand in a "stop" position at the same time. Some people use the word, "Enough!" to accomplish the same thing. Keep eye contact with your dog. Repeat this practice as often as needed over a week, possibly engaging the help of a friend or family member to knock on the door or ring the bell so you can take time for training. Within a week or less, your dog will stop barking after the initial warning bark. You can also use the tie-down (see Chapter 5) or the crate (see pages 106–7) if your dog is barking excessively while you are present.

Some pup parents have had their dogs debarked through surgery. We believe that is an extreme measure that could most likely be avoided by using the other suggestions we've given. We hope you will never take such drastic measures.

If dogs could talk, we think they might say: "Thanks for reviewing Dog 101. You already have an A+ from me."

Remember that Pop Quiz?

Consider this your review. If you've been paying attention, you can get a perfect score *and* be a great pup parent. All you have to answer is true or false.

1. If a dog is AKC-registered, I don't have to worry about genetic defects.

    TRUE   FALSE

2. Small dogs should be carried instead of walked.

    TRUE   FALSE

3. My dog's feces is biodegradable.

    TRUE   FALSE

4. Most dogs dislike long walks.

    TRUE   FALSE

5. There is no need to fence my yard if my dog and I have attended obedience training.

    TRUE   FALSE

6. I should let my dog have a litter of pups before I spay her.

    TRUE   FALSE

7. Dogs are safest riding in the car in their parent's lap.

    TRUE   FALSE

8. My dog must sleep in my bed to prevent separation anxiety.

    TRUE   FALSE

9. A barking dog is a sign of virility.

    TRUE   FALSE

You've already guessed that the answer to all of the questions is false, correct? If not, a little review may be in order. If you said false to all the questions, give yourself an A for Dog 101.

CHAPTER 5

ARE PUPPIES TOO LITTLE FOR PARENTING?

"There is no psychiatrist in the world like a puppy licking your face."

—Bern Williams

Who can look at a litter of puppies and not fall madly in love? Puppies are so tiny, fluffy, helpless, and just plain old cute. They are like little Norman Rockwell paintings, full of possibilities. Have you noticed that even pictures of puppies can put you in a brain-dead state where you don't even think about what's involved in raising them? Unfortunately, too often, pup parents think the adorable pup is too little to learn because he is just a baby. That attitude can only cause numerous problems for you and your dog later on. From the day you bring your dog home, it's time to begin parenting your pup.

We don't mean to piddle on your parade, but your new puppy *will*—to say nothing of chewing, biting, barking, etc. You can avoid a rude awakening and be prepared for your new bundle of joy if you try the following before bringing a puppy home:

Before you go to bed, pour apple juice on the carpet in several places and walk around in the dark. Set your alarm for the middle of the night, and go outside when it is cold and raining and plead, "Be a good puppy. Go potty. Now!" In the morning, cover all your clothing and furniture with dog hair and float some in your first cup of coffee. Before you leave for work, put chocolate pudding on the carpet and don't clean it till you come home at the end of the day. Leave your underwear in the living room and shred one of your shoes. As you walk out the door, take a screwdriver and gouge the leg of your table. Upon returning home from a hard day's work, turn on the TV, get comfy, and then, stand up shouting, "No, no! Do that outside!" Miss the end of your program. Finally, take a nice, warm blanket from your dryer and wrap it around yourself. This is how it feels to have your puppy fall asleep in your lap.

Is it worth it? Of course. Being prepared only enhances your joy because you won't have to experience any surprises or disappointment, and your puppy won't have to experience your wrath or any loss of love.

The Basics Before Bringing Home Puppy

If you were having a baby, you wouldn't go to the hospital, deliver the baby, and come home without any advance preparation. It's the same when you decide that adding a puppy to the family is right for you. Although we've covered a lot about preparing for a dog in previous chapters, we want to review it again here for those of you who think it might be different when the dog is so small and helpless. You can avoid some costly annoyances (if that is what you would call having your best pair of shoes destroyed) by puppy-proofing your house.

All kidding aside from the previous scenario, here's what you *really* need to do before you bring your pooch (whether puppy or adult dog) home. First, remove temptations that Junior might chew and ruin or chew and end up sick from. Then, create a system for confinement. Many pup parents like the crate method. Some use an exercise pen. Others find that a baby gate or playpen works fine. You may have the perfect room in your house ready for the new pup to hang out when you're not around to supervise. This room inside the house should be small, uncarpeted, with a door you can shut. Some kitchens, bathrooms, or laundry rooms fit this description.

As for supplies, you'll need dishes for water and food. You can use anything from a basic bowl to a designer dish. Plastic isn't easy to keep clean, and puppies love to chew on it, so we recommend heavy pottery or metal. You'll have to decide what kind of food you want to feed your baby. Again, the choices range from premium dry dog food to canned to raw to gourmet meals. It's up to you, but whatever you start with is probably what your pooch will come to expect, so think long-range before you choose.

But whatever you decide, make sure the dog food is premium food without additives, chemicals, or fillers. An informative article by the Animal Protection Institute was eye-opening about the way dog food is made and the number of additives that may or may not be safe. On their Web site, they provide a list of twenty-six additives and another list of diseases that have been traced to commercial products, including digestive problems, urinary tract diseases, blindness, heart disease, bone and joint diseases, and kidney failure. You wouldn't raise a baby on junk food, but you might be raising your pup on the dog food equivalent. We recommend that you do some research before deciding what to feed your dog.

Add to your supply list a collar, ID tag (or subdermal chip), a light leash, and bedding. Of course you'll need toys, tennis balls, and bones. Don't forget a bag of special treats that you use only for training purposes, like a stick of Rollover or the equivalent. If dogs could talk, they'd recommend that you cook up chicken gizzards, but it's really not necessary.

Health care starts immediately. Make an appointment with a veterinarian to get off to the right start with vaccinations, flea treatments, checkups, and medication for heartworm prevention. Don't forget to schedule that appointment for spaying or neutering before your pup reaches six months of age. You'll have a long relationship with your veterinarian, so if you aren't impressed by the person or the premises, shop around till you find someone you like and trust. We also recommend pet insurance (see page 61), but that's an individual choice. At least check it out because it can save you in the long run if your dog ends up with medical conditions you can't even think of when your baby is a cute and adorable puppy. Don't forget that gallon of carpet cleaning solution (we like Nature's Miracle), for the obvious.

Given how much you'll need for the new baby, you might want to consider holding a puppy shower. Invite all your friends and include a list of essentials as gift suggestions. Of course, you can shop for all of these items at a variety of stores or online, but wouldn't it be fun to have a big party to help you welcome your new baby to the family? We wonder which pet company will create a gift registry first. But enough of this crass materialism. On to the more important aspects of being a pup parent: puppy management.

> If dogs could talk, we think they might say: "I like the idea of a dog shower, but I'd rather have my very own birthday party, complete with cake and candles and a nice leg of lamb. Now that's worth waiting for a whole year!"

Parenting Your Puppy—Common Issues

Training a puppy is less painful when it is a matter of *doing* instead of *undoing*. Parenting puppies is like writing on a blank page. It's a common misconception, even among many professionals, that you must wait until a puppy reaches six months of age to start training, but there's been a great deal of new knowledge and understanding in this area. The optimal learning time for a puppy is before twenty weeks of age (five months). After that, it's primarily a matter of unlearning and undoing the bad habits and behavior patterns that have been allowed to establish themselves.

Puppies learn from their environment from the time they are three to four weeks old. It is crucial that a human is there to guide that learning, especially after seven to eight weeks of age. Up until then the puppy's mother and littermates do most of the teaching. We want to point out again that if you remove a puppy from his mother and siblings before the puppy is seven to eight weeks old, that puppy misses the opportunity to learn necessary social skills from them that cannot be taught by a human. This is one of the reasons we stress the importance of buying a puppy from a responsible breeder who is knowledgeable in these matters.

Puppy management and education is a process that takes time and commitment. Everyone has different priorities and questions about puppies, but there seem to be four common issues that canine parents struggle with: mouthiness and oralness (biting behavior), pestiness, destructiveness, and housebreaking. Some typical scenarios sound like this:

BITING: One doggy parent complained that her puppy was biting her excessively and aggressively, and that every time she tried to discipline her by pinning her to the ground and saying no, the pup got more aggressive and became very defensive. The biting got worse. Every time she walked across the floor, her pup pounced on her and grabbed her pant leg and started pulling her around, growling ferociously. A puppy who has been taken away too early from his littermates often has no ability to control nipping and biting behavior. This isn't necessarily a sign of aggression and dominance, but more a lack of ability to inhibit biting because the puppy never had a chance to learn the skills of bite inhibition by interacting with his own species.

PESTINESS: Another very common complaint is the puppy who cries and cries and whines and whimpers at night until allowed to sleep in bed with Mom and/or Dad. During the day, the same puppy wants to be petted constantly and won't take no for an answer.

DESTRUCTIVENESS: With larger puppies, complaints often involve the dog digging up parts of the yard or eating parts of the house. Sometimes they chew on decks, the siding, the latticework, or inside the house, eating parts of the furniture or carpets.

HOUSEBREAKING: Many pup parents complain about their pup soiling the carpet in spite of constant corrections with the rolled-up newspaper. "Accidents" of all kinds enrage and upset puppy parents who want their dogs housebroken properly. Their ineffective efforts at correction usually involve punishment: hitting the dog with a newspaper, rubbing the dog's nose in her messes, scolding loudly and telling her what a bad dog she is, and even hitting the dog with their hand. The dog responds to these corrections by hanging her head, slinking out of the room, looking like she has something to hide, and when no one is looking, repeating the same problem behavior.

Most puppy management problems, including the scenarios just described, are a result of a common mistaken belief that the right thing is to let the puppy run through the house, exploring and investigating at will, giving him all the freedom he wants. The puppy may be having a good time doing this, but he is learning every waking minute—whether you are there or not to direct his learning. By giving him this freedom in your home, he will learn many things that will make him happy in the moment but won't necessarily make you happy in the long run. What may seem like cute puppy behavior is often viewed as very annoying when it becomes adult behavior.

If you allowed your puppy to engage in undesirable behavior for a while, you may now feel it necessary to punish him to correct his behavior, but it's too late to be effective. Since your puppy already got away with performing the behavior in the first place, it's now an established behavior and has become a habit. When you aren't available to correct behavior when it happens, a vicious cycle will develop: Your puppy makes a mistake in your absence and you punish after the fact.

No one enjoys being around an unruly pet. You do your little ones an injustice if you let them learn behaviors that will get them in trouble at a later date. Instead of following your pup's lead, savvy pooch parents set safe limits, boundaries, and routines, using kind and firm follow-through, that help their little guys behave in acceptable ways.

Using the Pup Parenting Plan to Deal with Biting

Tucker was a three-month-old pug, weighing in at three pounds. He was adorable with his little Martian-like head. He was so much fun to play with, except for his bad habit of biting the hand that fed him. Of course it wasn't only the hand that he bit, but the pant leg, the arm, or any other piece of his mommy, Ruth, that he could get his little mouth around. Ruth knew that Tucker was a baby and that babies explore the world by biting. She also knew that Tucker was only playing, but his biting was troublesome to her and downright annoying to her friends who were refusing to play with him. She was getting pressure from them to be a better disciplinarian, and although she didn't agree with their suggestions of swatting him or grabbing his nose, or in one case, biting him back, she wasn't sure what to do. Yelling at him to stop had little effect, as did giving him other objects to chew and bite. The Pup Parenting Plan helped her find a workable solution. Here's how she answered the five questions:

1. The behavior that bothers me: My puppy won't stop biting me. Tucker's biting seems excessive. My other dogs didn't act this way. I'm wondering if he has more serious problems.

2. Why change is needed: Some of my friends have young children who are afraid to get near Tucker, and rightly so. I don't want one of them to get injured, nor do I want my friends to dislike Tucker. My methods aren't working, either, and I need to find a way to break him of this habit.

3. The mistake I am making: I have no idea.

4. A list of possible solutions:

- I could stop playing with Tucker until he stops biting. I could take him for walks and let him play at the dog park but refuse to play with him in ways where my body is near his.

- I could try ignoring him when he bites.

- I could cry when he bites.

- I could sign us up for puppy school or hire a trainer to see if there are suggestions I haven't discovered. I could read more about biting to find ideas I haven't tried.

5. Choose a solution and follow through: Ruth did some more reading and came across information about ignoring and how to do it. Since that had been one of her thoughts already, she was glad to see she was on the right track. She fine-tuned her approach by getting tips on how to ignore.

Whenever Tucker bit her, she stood up and walked away, saying calmly, "Tucker, we'll try again later." Her words were mostly for her, but she swore that Tucker understood everything she said, because after doing this for a day, he gave up biting her when she played with him. After walking away from Tucker, she'd go about her work, paying him absolutely no attention, no matter how much he whimpered or walked underfoot. The minute he stopped pestering her, she sat down on the floor, called him, and began playing again. If he bit, she repeated her solution, standing up, walking away, and calmly saying, "We can try again later."

Ruth had a backup plan, but she never had to use it. If walking away hadn't worked, and Tucker then started biting her legs, she was going to put him in his crate with a chew bone, saying, "We can try again later." Then she would wait fifteen minutes to a half-hour and repeat the entire cycle.

In addition to using ignoring to solve Tucker's biting, Ruth also made sure that he had plenty of toys and baited bones that he could chew on. Tucker easily distinguished between chewing on Mom and chewing on his dog toy.

Beware of Methods that Seem Like Play

Many of the methods suggested for letting your dog know that you are the boss fall flat with pups because they think you are playing with them. If you watch a litter of puppies play together, you'll notice that they bite each other, growl at each other, and roll around like little bear cubs. When you use methods that involve shaking, growling, grabbing, and lunging, you look like an overgrown puppy. Your pup is undoubtedly thinking, "Let the play begin!"

Though ignoring worked for Ruth and Tucker, there are many behaviors you can't improve by ignoring, either because your pup will learn the wrong lesson or the situation will get worse. But ignoring is perfect for a biter because your pup wants to play and be physically close to you. She will modify behavior quickly to have the chance to be with Mom or Dad.

> *If Tucker could talk, what would he say? "My mom is so smart. She figured out how to play with me and teach me that she's not for biting. Good thing she still likes it when I lick her, cuz she sure is tasty."*

Ignoring: A Tool that Works with Pesky Dogs

If you have a dog who is constantly nudging your knee, lifting your resting hand, standing next to you panting or whining, you've probably inadvertently been giving any kind of attention that your pooch would consider rewarding—meaning that your behavior serves as an incentive to frequently repeat the behavior you don't like. For many behaviors, ignoring is very effective because it involves giving the puppy no attention whatsoever.

Negative attention is better than none, so you may be unintentionally engaged in training that will create a dog you will learn to dislike. There is no room in kind and firm discipline for reprimands or commands such as "No," "Bad dog," or "Be quiet." All your pup is learning by these negative reprimands is that you are noticing him. Grabbing the puppy's nose and holding it closed, or popping the puppy under the chin, or grabbing the skin on both sides of the ears and shaking (commonly known as a scruff shake) are all forms of punishment and abuse. The puppy gets what he wants, which is attention, albeit negative attention. What he wanted was somebody to acknowledge his existence, and he got it. Therefore, you ended up reinforcing the very behavior you want to eliminate.

Overindulgence Can Cause Problems

As traumas go, you could prevent a large number of behavioral problems as well as a dysfunctional relationship between you and your dog if you don't indulge in overpetting and overstroking. No one wants to think that too much love could be a bad thing, but when your dog abuses your love and becomes a pest to get your attention, and you give in to his demands, you have trouble in the making.

Overpetting and overstroking occurs when the petting and stroking is initiated by your dog and given by you for no good reason. You may think that your personal enjoyment is enough reason, but it is not healthy for you or your dog when you become the trainee instead of the trainer. Often your dog has trained you so well that you are completely unaware of how you are responding to your dog's behaviors. The manipulating techniques your dog uses to bring about *your* training include nudging a hand or an elbow, pawing, whining or other distracting noises, leaning up against your leg, and/or intense eye contact.

We're not saying you should stop petting your dog. We are, however, saying you should avoid petting and stroking your dog when he asks for it and demands it, especially if the demands are excessive. One of the simplest preventive measures is to shorten the times you do pet your dog to five to ten seconds at a time, and refrain from petting unconsciously. In this way, you stop rewarding your dog for obnoxious behavior that you may later come to dislike intensely. You also avoid running the risk of creating an "addiction" with your dog, who can't live without constant touching. Too much petting can accidentally create separation anxiety, not to mention that doing it takes away an opportunity for your pup to receive encouragement (petting) for a job well done.

Here's how to break your dog of this demanding habit. When your dog walks up to you, nudges your hand, looks at you with those pleading eyes, or paws you to get your attention, and your hand obediently stretches out to pet her, hesitate for a moment and then ask yourself, "Why am I petting my dog right now?" If it's simply your bad habit, either ignore your dog while holding your hands tightly to your sides, put your dog on a tie-down, or get up and walk away and try again in a few minutes. Amazingly, a pesky little lap dog we know stopped her attention-seeking behavior in less than a day, once her Mom used these techniques.

We usually run into major problems when we introduce ignoring, because it is human nature to take some action when you think your little darling is misbehaving. Here's how the logic goes. "Rover is misbehaving. I need to tell Rover what not to do. Otherwise, how is he going to learn to behave? I have to show Rover who's boss." But what we want everyone to understand is that ignoring *is* doing something. It is helping your puppy learn how to belong to the family in socially acceptable ways. In most attention-getting behaviors, if the puppy doesn't get his behavior reinforced by getting the attention he wants, the behavior will fade out right away. This goes for all attention-getting behaviors: crying in the crate, scratching and crying at the back door, throwing himself against the door, eliciting affection by leaning up against you, or pawing on your knee or leg to get petted.

Often, parents of canine kids believe these attention-seeking behaviors are genetic within the breed, but most often the behaviors are taught inadvertently by the parents. One canine mommy described one of her two beagles in the following way. "Abby always has to have her way. She'll yap till she gets her way, whether it's for you to open the closed gate, pick her up, or get her food faster. If you aren't quick in the kitchen, she'll run and slam into the counter and then bounce off the cabinet door until you put her food on the floor. She's kind of like her daddy who always wants his way. She's just more overt about it."

Although beagles may have a reputation for cleverness, irritability, stubbornness, and phobias, her other beagle, Rocky, is completely different from Abby. He's more laid back and mellow, according to his mommy, although he's been known to be a clown from time to time. Unlike his sister, he waits patiently for Mom and Dad to feed him or pick him up, and shows none of the other characteristics of his twin sister.

What's the biggest difference, you may ask? How would you explain the different personalities in two dogs from the same litter living in the same home? Easily, says Mom. Her pooch daddy thinks Abby is just like him and so cute. He gives in to her every whim, just as he wishes his wife would give in to his. If his wife even looks cross-eyed at Abby, he picks up his canine kid, pets her, and says in baby talk, "Don't pay any attention to Mommy. She's just cranky from her day at work. You're a good doggy." He picked out Abby and Mom picked out Rocky, so each pooch parent gets to be the primary parent with a different dog. Mom does not accept misbehavior and is very firm and kind with Rocky, who behaves accordingly. (For more on dog personalities, see Chapter 8.)

Start Boundary Training Early to Nip Destructiveness in the Bud

Your puppy shouldn't be allowed any freedom in the house until he's been taught right from wrong and can be responsible for his actions. If you don't allow your puppy to make the mistake in the first place, it can't become an established behavior. Prevention is key.

Even though it is your puppy's nature to urinate, defecate, and chew things up around the house, he needs you, as the adult, to provide him with boundaries and structure. Puppies are looking for leadership as much as children are, and there can be serious ramifications without it. Living in a leaderless world can cause your dog to become anxious and tense and then participate in problem behavior as a way of relieving the tension.

A puppy with a dominant personality whose owner doesn't take on the job of leader will get the impression that when he gets to be a mature dog, he's supposed to be the designated leader. The consequences here can be aggression toward the owner, generally unruly behavior, and a dog that won't listen or take direction.

By now, you've probably played and cuddled with your new puppy, but have you established your leadership yet? The easiest way to do that is to begin setting boundaries using "confinement" and strict supervision. The plan varies by day or by night, but confinement is most easily done by using a crate and/or a tie-down. Confinement is the best cure for the problems related to destructiveness and housebreaking.

Although we have covered sleeping in your bed quite thoroughly in Chapter 4, we'd like to repeat ourselves here for those of you who are mostly concerned about training your new puppy.

Allowing your puppy to sleep on your bed in these early stages would be giving a very mixed message. Showing the pup that kind of equality leads to a confusing message. It says, "At night you are the same as us, but by day you need to switch gears and obey us, mind your manners, and do what we tell you." For a young dog who is learning about leadership, this can be confusing. For this reason, we recommend crating. If the crate is the right size, the puppy will not eliminate in it because it's against his nature to eliminate where he sleeps; if it's too large, he will use one part as the bathroom and the other part as sleeping quarters. Even if your puppy will be the size of a pony in another year, choose a crate that's appropriate for his size *now*.

At night, place the crate in your bedroom for bonding purposes. Many people are very surprised to hear that sleeping in your room at night is very significant for your relationship. The puppy, although he's sleeping, will get a strong sense of belonging if he's allowed to share the space with you. This is particularly true for owners who are working all day. You can't replace the time you spend sleeping with the puppy at night in the same room for building a strong bond. Remember that in nature, animals sleep in proximity to each other. As the pup gets older, he can handle more independence, including moving his sleeping place if either he or you decide to do that. If you take your lead from your dog, you may be surprised at the number of nights your dog falls asleep somewhere other than in your bedroom and doesn't want to be disturbed to move.

But while your dog is a youngster, it's important to have the crate in the bedroom so that you will wake up when the puppy wakes up with a need to go to the bathroom, which he will do at least once during the night if he is very young. If your puppy wakes up crying but doesn't have to go out, it is helpful to sit near the crate and pet your puppy briefly, comforting him with a soothing voice. You might think that doing this will teach your pup to cry for you, but the result is actually just the opposite. If you spend a minute or two reassuring your pup with sweet words and gentle touch, he will fall asleep—and let you sleep through the rest of the night. Think of how you might comfort a small child with, "There, there, it's okay. I'm here. You'll be fine. There, there little one." It will work with a puppy, too. Then return to your bed and allow the pup to settle back down.

Once the puppy sleeps through the night, if you don't want your dog sleeping in your bedroom, the puppy could sleep in a responsible older child's room; the next alternative could be the kitchen or the family room. The most important thing is that the puppy isn't shut in a small area or isolated away from the family. As we've said, if you take your lead from your dog, you may be surprised at how many pups are happy to move their sleeping quarters without a struggle.

Establish Daytime Boundaries for Your Puppy

Confinement during the day depends on how your home is set up. When you're not home, a puppy up to four or five months old should be confined in a kitchen, laundry room, or utility room with a baby gate, making sure the puppy has both water and an open-door crate available. It's generally not a good idea to leave the puppy in the back yard until he gets older, for safety reasons. If he is very little, he could find a place to get out, and there's always the risk of him being stolen, unless you take precautions. Keep in mind you have to puppy-proof the area, regardless of where he is, and remove anything that could harm him as well as things you want to keep safe from the puppy. Prevention is the goal here. We hear so many complaints about puppies destroying a home simply because it never occurred to the owner to put the dog in a smaller, dog-proofed space.

These confinement suggestions are examples of the mutual respect we refer to in the beginning of the book. For some people, it is easier to respect their dog than to respect themselves. For others, it is easier to respect themselves than to respect their dogs. This is not an either/or proposition; respect must go both ways to have a solid and special relationship with your pooch. You wouldn't be respecting yourself if you allowed your puppy to chew up the couch, leave puddles on the carpet, or shred your newspaper. On the other hand, you wouldn't be respecting your puppy by leaving her alone outside all day while you are at work or busy in the house. "Baby-proofing" your home is a way to practice mutual respect with puppies.

If you're gone for many hours, it would be good to have somebody come over, check on the puppy, take him out for a walk and playtime. Leaving a puppy alone at home all day is never an ideal situation. Review the information in Chapter 4 for ways to spend quality time with your dog. We advise people before they get a puppy to reconsider if they have to be gone eight hours a day, five days a week, since a lot of problems originate from that situation. As we've said, dogs are social by nature, and it's very difficult for them to be isolated from social contact all day. The learning process takes a lot longer under those circumstances, as opposed to someone being home all the time during your first three months together. It definitely makes a difference. Training can be done if you're not home during the day, but it does take more work and more patience. Don't be unrealistic about your expectations, and remember that rescue and adoption are always available if an older dog fits better with your lifestyle.

When you come home after being gone all day, you need to make up for the time you were not there by scheduling some special time that includes both mental and physical exercise for your puppy. Your pup has waited a long time for you, and like a child, needs your attention before you settle into reading the mail, watching the news, or making yourself a snack. You can also incorporate puppy management training practice during this time. Practice your sit, down, stay, come, and other cues as part of your puppy's daily routine. (See Chapter 6 for more information on improving communication through puppy management training.) This will provide the mental activity. For the physical activity we suggest playing with your puppy, throwing objects he can retrieve, playing hide and seek, and running on a fifty-foot line in an open space. Another alternative is to arrange for your dog to share playtime with a compatible puppy or adult dog or begin visits to the local dog park if you are fortunate enough to have one nearby.

There will be times when you are home that your puppy may need to be on a tie-down. This could be as simple as using a four-foot nylon leash to "umbilical cord" the puppy by tying the lead to a chair, your leg, a couch leg, a table leg, a door handle, or anything heavy enough that the puppy can't move. This is very effective, and it allows the puppy to be with you without getting into trouble or engaging in any unwanted behavior. Make sure he always has plenty of toys, especially animal products like pigs' ears and marrow bones. You can have a bed where he is tied up that moves when his tie-down moves. Every time you put him in a tie-down in a new spot, start by saying, "Go to your bed," or "Go to your spot." Then, give a food reward or praise so that the tie-down spot is always a pleasant place to go.

If your puppy whines and cries or barks when he is on the tie-down, you need to practice ignoring. As we've suggested, this is a very powerful behavior modification tool. In essence, it means do not speak, do not touch, do not look. When puppies cry and bark on a tie-down, they do it because they want attention. Regarding the notion of mutual respect, it is okay for your puppy to learn that he is part of the family, but not the center of the family. It is perfectly fine and natural for you to have some time for yourself, uninterrupted by demands from your puppy. You have shown respect to your puppy by giving him your full attention while you played, cuddled, taught commands, and ran around. Now it's your turn. If you do this repeatedly, your puppy will usually cease whining in a few minutes and begin chewing on a toy or baited bone, or fall asleep.

Puppies Thrive on Routines

Puppies learn much quicker in an environment where they know what to expect and when to expect it. Dogs are habitual. This is why it's important that you set up a routine that works for you. Lack of a regular routine can make a puppy insecure and confused and, in turn, can lead to other problems. Every household is slightly different, and not every routine works for everybody, so whatever routine you set up for yourself, you need to make sure it fits in with your lifestyle. Remember, the puppy is there to conform to your life, not the other way around.

Even so, keep in mind that you need to make certain adjustments in your life to comply with the needs of a very young puppy, such as frequent feedings, house-training, etc. You must make time in the routine you create for everything that is essential. Ideally, create times on a daily basis for some form of exercise: walking, running on a line in the park, playing with a friend's puppy in somebody's yard. Your puppy also needs special playtime involving you and the puppy together: doing a restraint exercise, brushing, massage, as well as quiet time on a tie-down on the puppy's "spot" where you do nothing but hang out together and bond without any physical touching. Feeding should be as regular as possible, depending on your work schedule, so you can regulate the puppy's elimination habits.

When you create routines, you are using a relational approach to problem solving. You are taking a leadership position by considering both your needs and the puppy's into account. There is rarely a need for the "old" kind of discipline (punishment) because following the routine eliminates most, if not all, power struggles.

We recommend that you go from three feedings a day to two at around fourteen weeks. That's when most puppies wean themselves off the third (midday) meal. Feed no later than five-thirty p.m., so your pup has plenty of time to empty bowels and bladders before bedtime, which varies from household to household. The important thing is that the puppy eliminates before you go to bed. Using this method, most puppies can usually go through the night at around ten to twelve weeks, assuming your day starts around five to six a.m. If not, don't worry. Many puppies still wake up around two or three a.m., at which point you need to take them out to go potty. This can go on until they are about four months old. A word of advice: make sure you are very calm and quiet when you take the puppy out at that time of the morning, and in no way give the puppy the idea that the day is supposed to be starting. Puppies wake up very quickly and can easily be led to believe, if you are acting at all in an excited way, that their day is starting and it's playtime at three in the morning. Be as quiet and calm as you can be and after the puppy eliminates, return the puppy to the crate.

How to Potty-Train Your Puppy

Some puppies are easy to potty-train. Others take more time. And then there are those who get off to a bad start at the kennel or with the backyard breeder. Such was the case with Marvel, a six- month-old cairn terrier who continued to have accidents on the carpet. If you have a dog like Marvel, or if you are looking for an effective method to potty-train your dog, here's what to do. First, you need to talk to your veterinarian to eliminate any medical reasons for problem behaviors, because nothing can change behaviorally if a dog is ill.

Next, limit your pup's freedom for up to three months, using a four-foot tie down, her crate, and an ex-pen. Put the ex-pen in an uncarpeted area (this prevents your dog from sneaking into another room to leave you a "surprise" as well as puddles on your carpets), using as many of the eight panels as you like. When you leave for work in the morning, put toys, animal products, a bowl of water, and her crate with open door in the ex-pen (your dog can use the crate to sleep in), and put your dog in the pen. Ideally, if you are going to be away for more than three or four hours, have someone come in and take her for a walk. If she urinates on the floor inside the ex-pen, the pen may be too large.

When you are home, put her on her walking leash and take her out to urinate. Both you and the dog walker need to use food rewards when she urinates. When you come into the house, put her on a four-foot drag lead and "umbilical cord" her to you or the furniture. In other words, she should never be out of your sight. Make sure you allow no more physical touching than you would normally. If she becomes a pest, step on the drag lead. Give her a sterilized bone with peanut butter or cream cheese so she gets busy with something. Not at any time is she allowed freedom in the house. If you go to the bathroom or take a shower, tie her to a piece of furniture or crate her.

If you catch your puppy urinating or defecating in the house, as quickly as possible and in a calm voice say, "Potty outside." Then move your dog outside to finish doing his or her business. If your pup doesn't go to the bathroom outside after about ten minutes, bring the pup back into the house and put him in the crate or confined area and try again in a half-hour. Repeat this till your pup gets the idea that outside is the place for potty.

You may be asking, "Why go to all this trouble? Why not just give her a whack with a rolled-up newspaper or squirt her with a spray bottle when she makes a mistake and be done with it?" Remember, we advocate kind and firm parenting as the best possible way to create a lifelong relationship with your pet that is respectful to both of you. Time for training puppies is intense and consuming, but the rewards are huge.

If puppies could talk, we think they might say: "Don't underestimate how much we can learn just cuz we're small. Show us what to do instead of punishing us for our mistakes, and we'll be the best dog you've ever had."

KIND AND FIRM PUP PARENTING PRINCIPLES

1. Puppies may be adorable, but they require much more time and effort than an adult dog. Make sure you are ready for that commitment.

2. Factor in the cost of supplies and veterinary care before buying your puppy. It could easily cost you more to care for your new pup than the initial purchase price.

3. Puppies are learning all the time, so make sure what they are learning is what you will be satisfied with as they get older. Don't put off training your pup.

4. Most problems with pups can be avoided by starting early boundary training and creating routines for training, including potty-training. You need to be physically present to train your pup.

5. Proper ignoring is more effective than any type of punishment. Make sure you and your pup know that mistakes are chances to try again.

CHAPTER 6

OBEDIENCE TRAINING: CREATE A COMMON LANGUAGE BETWEEN PUPS AND PARENTS

"'I want to go out!' 'I want something to eat!' 'Pet me, scratch me, rub my ears now!' Dogs go in for exclamation points."

—*Arthur Yorinks*, The Eyes Have It

Dogs aren't the only ones who go in for exclamation points. Just think how you sound when you're trying to get your dog's attention and you're being completely ignored. You know your dog isn't deaf because that same dog can hear you opening the refrigerator door from five rooms away. We know your dog has excellent hearing; after all, he is a dog. So how do you explain why that same dog experiences selective hearing when you say, "Come"? Maybe the refrigerator speaks your dog's language, and you don't.

On the other hand, like any pup parent, you know that your dog "talks" to you and is an excellent communicator. Dogs have different barks, growls, facial expressions, and behaviors for each occasion, and they use them until you get the drift. And they are very persistent conversationalists at that, as the Beck family discovered quite by accident one day.

Vicky and Andy and their four children thought they were very clever by giving a treat to their Yorkie, Sneezer, every time he wanted to potty outside. But what they couldn't understand was why Sneezer was getting so fat since they didn't feed him more than what the vet had suggested. It took them a while to learn that Sneezer was even more clever than they were. They eventually discovered that after one member of the family let him out and gave him a treat, he would soon find another family member and signal that he needed to go potty—and get another treat. Then he'd find someone else in his family and repeat the process. It took awhile to catch on, but one day, Vicki watched with fascination as Sneezer went outside, lifted his leg, and *pretended* to pee while Andy handed him his fourth treat in under fifteen minutes. Talk about being a convincing communicator!

In another family, Connie's half shih tzu–half Maltese, Sir Silky, demonstrated yet another example of how well dogs can communicate. According to Connie, Sir Silky has his own blankie—a towel that goes everywhere with him. He plays with it, sleeps with it, and waits patiently in the laundry room while it is being washed and dried. It is now frayed at the edges and pretty ratty. Connie tried to give him another, newer, nicer, blue towel, but he wouldn't have anything to do with it. He waited for "his" towel to come out of the dryer, and when it did, he grabbed it and ran off. Connie knows she better not take him to a doggy sitter without bringing his blankie. This dog certainly knows how to communicate effectively with his mom.

Like Vicky and Andy's Sneezer and Connie's Sir Silky, most dogs find a way to let you know exactly what they want. When they are standing next to the door, it's time to go outside. When they are pawing your leg while you watch a movie, they're ready to jump into your lap. When they come in from a walk and stare at the bowl on top of the shelf, they know it's where their treats are and they wonder if you'll remember it's time for one. When they start pushing their empty dish around, it's probably time for dinner. When you yell "Come" and they see something more interesting in a different direction and run that way, they are letting you know it's time for more training. Does this mean that dogs are better communicators than you? Could be. That's why it is important to participate in obedience training with your pup so the two of you can create a common language and learn to listen to each others' cues.

We know you talk to your dogs as if they were human, and we understand. That's what pooch parents do. We also know there are times that your pooches seem to understand you as well as you do them. They cock their heads and raise their ears and wag their tails, looking for the entire world as though they are interested in every word you have to say. But don't be fooled. There may be times when a conversation with your dog seems to do the trick, but there are other times when the language of action instead of words is what your dog needs to "hear."

We suggest you learn from your dogs and become as persistent, creative, and effective as they are so you can get—and keep—their attention. Obedience training is the best way to do that. Training isn't meant to create a master/slave relationship. Rather, it's a way of setting you and your dog up for success by learning a group of cues that you can both replicate almost automatically whenever needed. In other words, it helps you create a common language.

Obedience Training Has Many Benefits

Obedience training teaches you how to get your dog's attention in an effective and respectful way, while at the same time maximizing your dog's potential for understanding and delivering what you want and need. On top of that, when it's working, obedience training provides both of you with a great way to spend time together. The bonus comes when you or your dog can't seem to succeed at communication—you can use an obedience cue that both of you know and can do without thinking. For example, most dogs will sit when told, even if a delectable-looking canine of the opposite sex walks by. They are used to responding to this cue without hesitation because of the time you've spent training them. Using a familiar cue gets you centered as it gets your dog's full attention. By giving him a cue he has been taught to respond to in a specific way, you are giving him a *job* to do that distracts him from the undesirable behavior. This allows you to reward him for something he can succeed in doing, as opposed to scolding or correcting him for inappropriate behavior. Dogs can't obey an obedience cue and continue the bad behavior at the same time. Now the two of you are truly communicating.

Dogs thrive when they are with pup parents who know what they are doing. Most dogs have an inherent desire to serve and please, but it's up to you to learn how to bring those qualities out in your dog. The more you can replace frustration and anger with quiet calmness, the more effective you'll be. Obedience training helps you do just that. As you learn the cues and how to use them, you find ways to give a correction so that your dog doesn't feel intimidated or fearful. The message you are giving is, "Don't worry, I'll help you learn. I have everything under total control, and it's going to be alright."

Do You Need Help with Obedience Training?

Some people will be very effective teaching their dogs how to walk without pulling on the leash and lunging at other distractions. Others may have no problem helping their dogs learn to sit, stay, come when called, or go to their spot/bed/rug. Still others will want and need help. There are several options. There are group classes, usually offered regularly by individual trainers, training clubs, community colleges, or sometimes through the local parks and recreation department. You might even use a training video. Your choice will depend on your personality, your dog's personality, your parenting style, your checkbook, and your available time. Some newspapers have a special classifieds section just to help you find the right training program for your dog. You can check with your veterinarian, the Yellow Pages, online, or talk to other pooch parents and ask where they went for obedience training. Just make sure the program is nonpunitive.

Another option is a board-and-train program, where your dog is kept for several weeks at a training facility (see Chapter 9 for details). If you have a dependent and/or dysfunctional relationship with your dog, an in-kennel program may be best for you. Even if you are reluctant to send your dog away for two weeks, you'll find that she will thrive by getting away from you and learning from someone else. The trainer will then teach you how to work with your dog at the end of the training. An added benefit is that you may be more inclined to follow through with practice once your pup comes home because you've spent a lot of money and also know that your dog has worked hard for the past two weeks to learn something new.

You could also hire a private trainer to come to your home and work with you and your dog. Many people are under the mistaken impression that when they hire a private trainer, their own involvement will be minimal and passive and that the trainer will fix the dog and deliver the obedient pup as a finished product. But success is based more on what you as the pup parent do with the information and instructions given you by the trainer. To get maximum benefits from an in-home trainer, once you're shown how to work with your dog, you'll need to practice, practice, practice.

Six Traps That Defeat Successful Dog Training

Regardless of where you get your instruction, pay special attention to the six traps that defeat successful dog training.

1. Inconsistency. A cue should mean only one thing every time you say it. "Sit," for example, means just that—not "stand," not "down." Be consistent, or your dog will become confused and learn to ignore you. A lack of consistency and lack of a clear, concise approach have been known to lead to defensive aggression.

2. Giving a cue without being able to enforce it with a correction. If you can't enforce the cue, don't use it! Each time you give your dog a cue you can't enforce instantly, you are teaching him that if he doesn't want to, he doesn't have to do what you are requesting.

3. Giving a cue more than once. "Sit, sit, SIT!!!" As it does with children, nagging teaches your dog to tune you out. Give your dog one chance to respond, and if he chooses not to, give an immediate correction depending on the method you are using, followed by a treat or verbal encouragement.

4. Improper leash handling. One of the hardest things to teach most doggy parents is proper leash handling and how to use the leash (or long line) for corrections. Watch first-time canine parents walking their dog and notice how they use the leash to drag, pull, or choke their baby. Not only is the method ineffective, it's also cruel.

5. Failure to encourage at the right time. Encouragement is absolutely essential if you want a dog who works happily and willingly. Don't take his good responses or desired behavior for granted. Let your dog know, with lavish and sincere physical and/or verbal encouragement, when he pleases you. Encouragement should be sincere and calm, not overemotional or gushy.

   Motivational methods such as tidbits, petting, and use of a ball or toy as encouragement are so much more effective than force and compulsion. Encourage your dog to enjoy his work. Ideally, his tail should be up and maybe even wagging when you work with him.

6. Incorrect tone of voice. Your voice must sound authoritative but never angry or upset. Use a strong voice, but not a loud one, unless when using the recall and your dog is far away from you. Keep your voice

happy and enthusiastic. Dogs love hearing, "Good job. Atta boy (or girl)!"

Obedience training is only *one* aspect of parenting your pup, however. In some ways, it's like teaching your child good manners and other social graces. We've discovered that methods evolve and change. And just like parents of children, pup parents tend to be very successful using a little of several different methods coupled with what they watched their parents do when they were kids. We are not promoting any one method for obedience training in this book. What we are promoting is nonpunitive, mutually respectful obedience training that is applied with consistency and love.

If you decide to go with a trainer, do keep in mind that depending on which book he or she read, they may be dogmatic and insist that there is only one way to train your dog. But since positive dog training has become the norm these days, you will likely have your pick of encouraging methods. In *The Only Dog Training Book You'll Ever Need*, Gerilyn J. Bielakiewicz says, "You should never use any training method that makes you feel uncomfortable because you think it might hurt your dog…. If you're positive a technique won't do any harm, but you're just not sure if it will work, go ahead and try it to see for yourself." We couldn't agree more. If your dog isn't responding, it's simply not the right method for either of you. Move on to something else.

What Equipment Enhances Your Efforts?

Depending on the book you read or the class you take, there will be differences in what is suggested as the proper equipment. The kind of training equipment you use and how you use it will make a big difference in how successful you are going to be working with your dog. A doctor can't perform surgery without special instruments and your mechanic can't repair your car without good quality tools. Dog-training equipment (collars including Haltis, Gentle Leaders, and other head collars, leashes, and lines) must be effective, safe, functional, and comfortable for your hands.

The training collar you use depends on your dog's temperament and trainability. There are three different types: the curb link choke collar (sometimes referred to as a slide collar), the pinch collar, and the head collar. Contrary to popular belief, a *pinch collar* is often more humane than a *choke collar*, provided it is used correctly. By "correctly," we mean that you are trained by a professional who makes sure that your dog won't be abused by the collar and that your dog responds to one little jerk instead of constant and regular jerking of the collar. You get maximum results with a minimum amount of force simply by giving a quick jerk of the leash. Even the gentlest training guides we reviewed talked about the need for a properly used pinch collar on some dogs. The *head collar* looks and works a lot like a horse halter and can be very effective on strong, insensitive dogs who do not respond well to a neck collar. The technique you use with a head collar is quite different from a choke or pinch collar. Here, you are giving a light pull on the leash, which results in turning your dog's head in your direction. It's a surefire attention-getter without using force of any kind.

One drawback to a head collar is that, to the uninformed, it resembles a muzzle because of the strap that goes over the nose, although it in no way restricts the dog's ability to open his mouth. Often people approaching a dog with a head collar are afraid because they think your dog is dangerous and wearing a muzzle. Many dog parents feel upset that someone would think badly about their dog, and some even stop using this excellent piece of training equipment because of the misunderstanding. We suggest that when people ask if your dog is wearing a muzzle, simply say, "This is called a head collar. It's used for training dogs that don't like to be jerked by the neck. My dog is comfortable wearing it, and she is a perfectly friendly dog." Parents of any kind don't like to think that others dislike their baby.

A word of warning: The pinch or curb link choke collar must never be left on your dog when he is alone, both outside and inside the house. It can kill him if he gets stuck or trapped because there is no way your dog can release the choking motion of the collar by himself. Never tie up your pooch on a choke or pinch collar, even if you're present, for the same reason. If your dog starts pulling on his rope or chain to get closer to you or to chase an animal, the weight of his body against the collar can strangle him. Use a nylon or leather buckle collar for tying or for when he is alone. You can attach his identification tag and rabies tag to that collar. Do not put tags on a training collar!

In *The Guide to Beginning Obedience*, Nikki Moustaki suggests replacing choke collars and prong collars with a harness and nylon collar because "...most puppies will respond well to positive reinforcement training and won't need severe corrections on their sensitive necks." Bielakiewicz encourages pooch parents to use the head halter, with a caveat that "no one device is right for every dog." Not only do we agree with this statement but we would add that dogs who are overcorrected or severely treated usually require retraining to rid them of their bad habits.

But what good's all this talk about collars if you haven't found the proper leash? Your *training* and *walking* leash are one and the same. This leash should be six feet long and about ⅝-inch wide, made of either cotton web or leather. These materials are strong, flexible, and hand-friendly, giving you a firm, comfortable grip. Nylon leashes have a tendency to burn or cut your hands. Some are also much too thick and clumsy with large, heavy snaps. Good training equipment should be as lightweight and as inconspicuous as possible.

Use a forty- to fifty-foot-long line made of either ⅛- or 3/16-inch-thick parachute cord for practicing the recall command that we covered in Chapter 4 and for exercise. Most hardware stores or outdoor stores carry it, and you can also find many choices on the Internet. We recommend that you use a pair of thin leather gloves when you work with the long line because it can cause rope burns if you need to give a line correction. Since the line can also get wrapped around your ankles and legs, you might be more comfortable in long pants. Please don't ever tie your dog up with the long line, as it is not safe. If your dog ever needs to be tied, use a ready-made plastic-coated aircraft cable. (See Chapter 4 for information on tying up your dog safely.)

Although you see many pup parents walking their dogs on retractable leads, we don't recommend using them for training, as they can be extremely unsafe for some owners. People with poor reflexes and balance can fall when taken by surprise by their dog moving quickly toward a stimulus. You have next to no control of your dog with this device, especially if your dog is large, making it practically impossible to do any type of training exercise. The retractable leash works well if you are on a hiking trail or walking where you want to give your dog a little more freedom to sniff and follow scents, but still not have him off-lead. If your dog is older and/or voice-trained, the retractable leash isn't a problem.

Your Dog Can Walk without Pulling

We want to stress that this chapter isn't a substitute for obedience training. You and your pup need to get involved, learn, and practice together to get communication going smoothly. When you decide on a program, since there are many choices, make sure that the one you choose is respectful, positive, nonpunitive, and kind.

Here's a preview of how several different programs approach teaching you to walk your dog. Is one better or more right than the other? We don't think so. We've chosen these four because they have a lot in common and meet the requirements of firmness and kindness. You'll have to be the judge of which is best for you and your dog.

Method 1: Therry's Technique

Put on your dog's training collar and clip on a six-foot leash. Give the cue: "Buster, let's go." Immediately after saying it, begin walking at a brisk pace. Your dog should always be on your left side and should not be allowed to cross over in front of you. It is okay if he walks a few steps behind you. Do not, however, let him pull ahead of you. Hold the "handle" end of the leash in your right hand in front of you, close to your waist area. You can pick up the slack in the leash with your left hand, but the sign of correct walking is a completely loose leash, with no tension or tightness.

For those of you using a head collar, the technique is a little different than if you use a pinch or curb link collar. The corrective jerks are not as forceful and there is more of a guiding action. With other types of training collars, you want a loose leash; with the head collar, you may need a *slight* tension in the leash if your dog is a heavy puller. What you don't want to do is pull your dog around or force your pup in any way. Once again, put the "handle" end of the leash in your right hand and use your left hand to pick up the slack. If you find any part of this information in any way confusing, *sign up for an obedience class or work with a trainer*. It is more important that you teach your dog (and yourself) correctly from the start than to create bad habits you'll have to break later. If you have already trained a dog, the directions in this section will sound very familiar. But again, this chapter is not intended to replace obedience training.

When you practice your walking, incorporate three things to keep your dog on his toes: right turns (180-degree pivot to the right), left turns (180-degree pivot to the left), and halts (stop and sit by your side). To keep your dog from pulling ahead and to correct him if he does, you can do a quick right turn or a quick jerk-release with the leash, snapping straight back as you say "Easy." Step up toward the dog to create slack in the leash before you jerk, as it's impossible to jerk a tight leash. Use your left hand for the jerk, letting go immediately after the jerk. If you are constantly jerking your dog, you are using either the wrong technique or the wrong equipment. Some dogs are so reactive to a jerk that you rarely have to do it more than once or twice *in the dog's lifetime* to get her attention. If your dog isn't as responsive, or if you find yourself jerking constantly, for more humane and respectful training, we advise that you use a head collar.

To prepare your dog for the right turn, say his name, wait one or two seconds while you are still walking, then say, "Let's go," and pivot to the right and continue walking in the opposite direction. If your dog hasn't been paying attention, he'll have to speed up a little to catch up with you. Give lots of verbal praise or a treat once your dog is walking at your side. On the left turn, your dog is on your inside. Before you make this turn, make sure your pooch is close to your leg and not ahead of you. The cue is, "Buster, move." Begin your left turn and keep walking while shortening up on the leash. He will figure out how to get out of your way and walk at your side. Practicing right and left turns is an excellent exercise to get your dog to pay attention and listen carefully to you.

Several times during the walk, practice your halts, having your dog sit by your side when you stop. Help him sit as straight as possible, parallel to your left leg. First, say his name to get his attention and alert him that something is about to happen. Then take two or three steps, slowing down, and then stop and say, "Buster, sit." Just as you say, "sit," twist your upper body at the hips to the left, looking at the dog's rear over your shoulder. Your left arm swings back along with your shoulder and ends up pointing at your dog's rear. Your dog does not see the hand, but he sees the sloping angle of your shoulder, which helps him sit straight.

Many pup parents are tempted to teach their dog to sit by pulling up on the leash and pushing down on their dog's rear end. You do not need to do either. By using the motion we've described, you don't have to pull the leash up or push the butt down. Praise her verbally and/or pet her quietly on the head when she is in a good sit.

It's your job to set the pace and the direction on your walk. Allowing your dog to pull you around is teaching him to be rude and disrespectful. Don't let your dog get the idea that he is walking you. When your dog starts pulling, the turns work wonders to get you back on track. Do take time to give your dog a chance to sniff around on the walk. Use the cue, "Take a break," and let your pooch move out on the leash. When you're ready to start walking again, say, "Buster, let's go," and start walking forward.

Therry's Technique is the method Lynn decided to use in the early 1990s with her Samoyed, Buddy, because it was so effective when she used it twenty years earlier with her Scotty-poo, Thumper. She and Thumper had attended obedience classes where she learned the method. It took only one sharp, quick jerk and she never had to do it again to get Thumper's attention or cooperation. You can imagine her surprise when she repeated the same method with her Samoyed, who interpreted the jerk of his leash as a signal to start pulling her forward like a sled. The pinch collar was totally ineffective. When Lynn switched to the head collar, with the first gentle turn of his head, Buddy was a different dog. He paid attention, remained calm, and was very cooperative.

Method 2: Clicker Trainer

We include information here on clicker training because we think it is a very positive and humane way to obedience-train your dog, and it goes along well with what we are teaching pup parents in this book. It is kind and firm, proactive, and effective. Put on your dog's training collar and your twenty-five-foot-long line. Then, says Gerilyn Bielakiewicz, "Walk at a brisk pace and change direction frequently so that your dog has to pay attention to where you're going. The more you turn, the more your dog has to focus on you. Once you get the hang of walking and turning frequently, start to pay attention to the moment your dog turns to follow you, then click and treat him for catching up to you."

These directions might appear extremely simple, but we're not including all the advance work needed to practice shaping behavior, using lures, and marking events with the small hand-held clicker; nor are we covering the weaning process from lures and clicks. But if you are curious, the method bears further book study or finding a trainer who can teach you to use it.

Method 3: The Moustaki Method

Everyone who has ever trained a dog knows that you must first get the dog's attention. Nikki Moustaki talks about how she does that by letting a dog get completely tangled up in a long line. Once the dog has run out of line, she says, "give the line a snap and then move in the opposite direction again. Do not talk.... Each time your dog walks one way, you walk the other way. Continue this until every time you turn around, your dog follows you....

Once your dog watches for your next move and begins to follow you, praise him verbally and give him a treat." You can probably accomplish the same behavior following Method 1, but this may be a way of helping some dogs discover how to behave the right way without associating any corrections with you.

According to Moustaki, after you've done the attention-getting work, you should be able to get out your six-foot leash, attach it to the harness, put the dog on your left side, walk forward, and say, "Heel." If your dog pulls ahead, "simply stop and lure him back to your side with a treat."

Method 4: Positive Reinforcement

There are a group of trainers who use food treats and rewards as their primary training method. Among them are Brian Kilcommons and Sarah Wilson. Here's how they teach "Let's Go" in their book, *Good Owners, Great Dogs*. Start by "holding the lead in your left hand and a toy or a treat in the right. Tell [your dog], 'Let's go' and step off with confidence. Hold your right arm across your body so the treat or toy is held above and slightly in front of the pup's head. Encourage him to look up at you by teasing him a bit with the toy or treat. Speak excitedly, bob your hand up and down to get and keep his attention. When the pup looks up at you, praise him warmly. If he is distracted, squeak the toy, get his attention, and praise him.... After the pup has given you 20–30 seconds of attention, give him the toy or treat. Play a bit, relax, and then work again."

Additional Obedience Training Cues

Regardless of the method you choose to use to obedience-train your dog, make sure it includes training your dog to walk at your side, how to meet someone else on the trail, how to refrain from putting something in his mouth that could hurt him or that he could hurt, how to get your dog to come to you, and how to sit, lay down, and stay.

No matter how well-trained your dog is on a leash or long line, if you want to take your dog off-leash in an open area such as a park, field, or beach, once again, you really need to know your pooch. Some dogs would never run, while others will bolt at the first chance. (Refer to "Dog Groups and Breeds" on pages 76–77 in Chapter 4.)

Therry recommends using the following methods to expand your common language. Say, "Ah-ah, leave it!" instead of "no," which is widely misused and overused. The "Ah-ah," spoken with a guttural voice, gets your dog's attention immediately. The "leave it" cue is used when your dog is chasing, picking things up (before he puts the object in his mouth), chewing, sniffing, and losing attention while you are practicing walking, etc.

"Buster, give!" can be used when you want your pooch to give up something he has. Before you give the command, put your hand on the object. Look the dog straight in the eye. Now say, "Buster, give!" firmly and take the object. Use of your dog's name is important here.

The "Back!" cue basically means stop. You use it when you are going through a door or gate and your dog tries to go ahead of you. Your dog should be behind you. He can sit, stand, lie down, or walk away, but he cannot walk forward. "Back" should never be confused with "stay." "Back" is also used in the car, before you invite him out with a "let's go." He should never be allowed to jump out of the car at will! Do not use the cues "sit," "down," or "stay" inside the car, as you will not be able to enforce them while you are driving.

"Off!" is used for any jumping action whether it be on you, somebody else, furniture, countertops, etc. Please remember not to give an "Off" cue if you can't back it up with a correction! Ideally, the correction should be given simultaneously with the cue.

Setting Up Time for Training

Once you have the correct equipment and an understanding of the cues, incorporate your dog's education (and yours, too) into your daily life as much as possible. *Practice* and *repetition* are two guarantees for success. Remember, you're both learning a new and common language, and new languages require lots of repetition to become comfortable and usable. You can practice the "Down, stay" in the house while you are going about some task. It's easy. The "Sit, stay" cue is perfect at the door when getting ready for a walk, or when you open the door to head for the car. Use the "Back" cue every time you are going through a door or gate and your pooch starts following you, but isn't going to be able to accompany you. Take your pooch for a walk in the neighborhood as often as you have time, practicing turns ("Let's go" and "Move") and "Sit" by your side. When you want him to come to you in the house or backyard, use your informal "Buster, right here." Praise lavishly when he comes. And please remember that practice time is different from the rest of the day, when your pooch is hanging out or playing with you.

If possible, take your dog to a park or open area (school playground, etc.) for a recall session as well as playtime and exercise. If you want him to respond well under all circumstances, it is extremely important that you work him with outside stimuli and distractions as much as possible. Training done in as many different locations as possible increases your dog's ability to respond to cues. Your dog will look forward to training time more than you can imagine.

A bored, hyperexcitable, and underexercised dog left alone for long periods of time almost always develops a problem behavior sooner or later! By taking your dog to a park to run off some steam, play with other dogs, retrieve a ball or Frisbee, or practice cues, you're adding years to his life while building a great relationship.

> If dogs could talk, we think they might say: "First dog says to second dog while waiting patiently in 'Down, stay' at obedience training class, 'I'd like to find the bozo who invented the choke collar and give him a snap or two.' Second dog replies, 'I agree. By the way, have you noticed how much people look like their dogs? I people-watch to make the time fly while I'm in one of these 'Down, stays.' Look at my mom. She's got the same squat, boxy body I have, and her hair hanging in her eyes looks just like mine. She must be very proud to look like me.'"

KIND AND FIRM PUP PARENTING PRINCIPLES

1. A common language is essential to having a well-behaved dog.

2. Obedience training is the best option for creating a common language.

3. Because there are many methods available, make sure the method you use is positive and nonpunitive.

4. Using the proper equipment can make obedience training a lot easier. The head collar is the best choice for a strong-willed dog.

5. Inconsistency and a lack of follow-through can defeat the best efforts.

6. Your dog will enjoy obedience training and look forward to that time with you.

7. In an emergency or when you feel out of control, ask your dog to sit, and then relax and breathe before starting up again. The "sit" cue seems to be the easiest for most dogs to learn and to remember and do.

CHAPTER 7

SOLUTIONS FOR THE ONGOING CHALLENGES OF PUP PARENTING

"Why is it always 'good dog'? Why can't it ever be great dog?"

—*Author Unknown*

Y ou're a kind and firm pup parent. You use the Pup Parenting Plan instead of reacting to your canine kid. You've done as much preventive maintenance as possible and have set up your living space to avoid problems. Your dog has been neutered or spayed, has a lovely fenced-in area to play in, goes on frequent walks, socializes at the dog park, and has passed obedience training with flying colors. Why, then, are you still having problems with your pup? Probably for the same reason parents of human children do. Just as soon as they get one issue sorted out and running smoothly, their children provide another challenging opportunity. It's the nature of having children, whether human or canine. Dealing with change is what keeps all parents on their toes and feeling alive. As with human kids, the minute you think everything is in order, be ready for your pup to present you with a new experience to test your parenting mettle.

This is the time when many parents resort to punishment. After all their hard work, they explain the problems in this way: "My dog knows the difference between right and wrong. Now she is testing me on purpose, defying my leadership." That couldn't be further from the truth.

Think back to Marley from Chapter 3, the dog who kept jumping up on the couch when his parents weren't home, only to be discovered when they came home and found a sticky note stuck on his butt? Did Marley "know" he shouldn't get on the couch? No. Marley knew what was pleasurable for him and what felt rewarding. The couch was soft and felt good. If Marley could jump on the couch and stay there without interruption, then he would. He didn't "know" he shouldn't. Your dog is like Marley.

To help you understand why dogs don't *know* what you think they know, consider another situation. Suppose you felt confident that your male dog was well trained to come when you said "Come," and to walk at your side when you said, "Rover, let's go." Would you still leave that dog off-leash if you were going to an area filled with female dogs in heat? We doubt it; so the next question is, "Why not?" The answer is obvious: because you know your dog is a dog with very strong dog instincts.

Dogs may be very intelligent, but it goes without saying that they don't think the way we do. Believing dogs can think and understand the way humans do creates a huge communication breakdown. Dogs will always follow their dog instincts when you aren't there. Dogs can learn basic cues and follow them as long as you are there to follow through, but don't expect them to do what you think they *know* when you aren't there. People who aren't wise enough to know that dogs don't understand "no" the way they think they do often spend hours of frustration trying to make their dogs understand things that simply aren't possible for them to understand. They create stress for themselves that they could avoid. They may also cause a lot of stress to their dogs by punishing them for things they can't comprehend. Not only is punishment a kind of communication that is disrespectful to your dog, it just plain doesn't work when you forget that a dog is a dog, thinks like a dog, behaves like a dog, and is capable of understanding only what a dog can understand.

Don't waste your time trying to use shame or guilt as motivators on your dog, either, because they are as useless as punishment. Margaret found this out with her cocker spaniel, Vicki. Margaret was very frustrated with Vicki and wondered, "Why does my dog go into the trash under the sink as soon as I get in the shower? She doesn't get into the trash when I'm around. Why does she go into my closet and get my underwear every time if I leave the closet door open? I've told her a million times not to do these things."

Margaret would try to shame Vicki into good behavior by saying, "Who did this? Bad dog!" The truth is that Vicki isn't a bad dog—she is a dog. Dogs do what works for them, not necessarily what works for you. Margaret expected her dog to understand more than she could comprehend. Guilt and shame may motivate some humans, but it has no place in parenting your pooch.

We are not saying that dogs should be allowed to do anything they want just because they don't understand. What we are saying is that in addition to all that you have done thus far, there is more to learn about pup parenting. We've talked about several of these parenting techniques throughout the first six chapters, but we'd like to refresh your memory and add new information. Our focus in this chapter is on methods that reduce your dog's opportunities to misbehave by using an ounce of prevention, the tie-down, routines, and/or setups. When used properly, they will eventually become obsolete because your dog will have learned to handle her freedom.

> *If dogs could talk about their lapses, we think they would say: "We know there are times you'll be angry with us and want to punish us. After all, you're only human! But please remember, dogs are for petting, not for hitting."*

An Ounce of Prevention Goes a Long Way

Margaret, the pup parent of Vicki the cocker spaniel, stopped feeling so stressed when she decided to use an ounce of prevention instead of guilt and shame. She limited Vicki's choices by remembering to shut her closet door. Then she placed a child protector clip on the trash cupboard door below the sink. Dogs understand this kind of nonverbal communication. When they experience a barrier, they give up the misbehavior and move on.

Here's how other families used an ounce of prevention. The Connor family used a crate for their dog at night until they were convinced she could make it through the night without having an accident. The Shermans put their big Lab on a tie-down whenever their grandbaby came to play so he wouldn't knock the baby over. The O'Donnells made sure that their pup stayed in the enclosed yard in the morning until the kids were off to school and Mom had time to take him for a walk. The Larsons stopped their escape artist from running out the door by putting him in the kitchen and shutting the door to the rest of the house whenever anyone was coming or going. The Mancuccis kept their dog on a leash as they walked him from the house to the car. And the Evers kept a baby gate in front of the stairs to the carpeted bedrooms their dog seemed to love to pee on. These simple procedures saved hours of problems and loads of aggravation.

The Drag Lead and Tie-Down Limit Choices

The drag lead and tie-down are two training devices that guarantee successful communication with your pup without the use of punishment. These methods are nonverbal, preventive, and have action-based follow-through. Both the drag lead and tie-down eliminate your dog's choices, narrow his world (confinement) for short lengths of time, and gradually introduce him to more freedom when he is ready for it. Not only will you have a good dog when you use these methods, you'll have a great dog!

A drag lead is a four-foot, heavy nylon cord that you attach to your dog's buckle collar every minute he is in the house. When your dog has a lead dragging from his collar, he immediately feels more responsive because of the weight the lead creates. Some dogs may at first get very excited because they associate the leash with going for a walk, but in a few days they will realize that the drag lead doesn't mean a walk is coming. Use a different leash for walking, preferably one made out of cotton or leather.

You may want to set up several tie-down spots in your house, including one in your bedroom. You can use a heavy piece of furniture or an eyebolt in the baseboard or wall. If your dog chews on her drag lead, use a four-foot-long piece of plastic-coated aircraft cable (found at home and garden stores, on the Web, and at many feed and pet stores) with a snap in each end: one for the eyebolt and one for the buckle collar. Put down a rug, folded comforter, or fleece bed to define the tie-down spot. You can move the bedding material from spot to spot, depending on which spot you are using. There should also be some of your dog's favorite toys or, if your dog is allowed, animal products (rawhide, hooves, baited femur bones) at the tie-down spot. Dogs, like children, do *not* have to suffer to learn. Their tie-down spot, just like a place for time-out, should be comfortable and have toys or distractions available.

Use the tie-down when you don't want your dog underfoot, when you have company, when your dog needs a time-out, when he needs to learn to accept being confined to one area—his own space—or if your dog needs to be reintroduced into the house after having been an outdoor dog. If your dog jumps up on counters, furniture, or laps, use this system instead of screaming a reprimand command or engaging in some form of punishment. Immediately, calmly, and quietly pick up the drag lead and simply "umbilical cord" your dog to you or to the furniture you are sitting in. Or, walk your dog to the nearest tie-down spot, click the drag lead to the eyebolt and walk away without saying a word.

A tie-down should never be used as punishment. Your dog won't perceive your behavior as punitive as long as you do not show anger or frustration when you place him on tie-down. In fact, there should be a pleasant surprise on the tie-down spot in the form of a baited bone or some other valued resource such as a favorite animal product not presented at any other time. It is time out from the activity that was taking place.

Using the tie-down is saying to your pup, through action, "Right now, I am not very happy with your behavior. You are not acting in a responsible way. What you're doing is not working for me and I don't want to be around you right now, so I'd like you to be over here on your tie-down so you and I don't get into a power play, a yelling match or any other type of game that neither one of us is going to win." And just think: all those ideas are nonverbal. Your dog hears what you are doing instead of "Blah, blah, blah, blah," and other meaningless noises that often spring from your mouth.

If your dog puts up a fuss by crying, barking, or lunging on his tie-down, completely ignore him. When you take him to his tie-down spot, your attitude should be: *This is something that needs to happen right now.* Most dogs eventually give up and quiet down. Wait approximately 30 seconds before you reinforce the now calm and quiet behavior. You can either walk up to him very quietly and present the food reward at the tie-down spot, say "good" quietly, and walk away, or, if you are a food thrower, you can toss a small piece of Rollover to him at his tie-down place. This is extremely effective, as he will figure out what works when the reward comes. Now you are establishing new behavior patterns.

It's possible that he will get up and start fussing again, and if he does, ignore, ignore, ignore. Reward intermittently, without petting if your dog is excitable. As an alternative to the Rollover, you can reinforce the good behavior by rebating the bone with an even more valuable substance like liverwurst (some dogs think this is better than candy), showing how much you appreciate calm and quiet and how well that will work for him. With a nonexcitable dog, you can walk up to the tie-down spot, sit down for awhile and let him lay his head in your lap. In other words, encourage him with your presence. For obvious reasons, make sure you never take him off the tie-down spot in the middle of any kind of noise or fussy behavior. You want your dog to know that fussing will not work.

Don't confuse the tie-down spot with the formal down stay command you will learn in obedience-training classes. Your pooch should never be asked to down stay at a tie-down spot. The whole purpose of the tie-down is that the dog is not under a formal command. You can use the phrase, "Go to your spot/your rug/your place," with the goal in mind that at a later point after practice and training, your dog will voluntarily approach his spot on your suggestion. Don't use the phrase, "Go lie down" if you intend to do any formal training with your dog, because that would interfere with your down stay and make it ineffective.

Your dog should stay on the tie-down for only a short time, and then you can try again to see if he will avoid the misbehavior that led to the tie-down. A few minutes is plenty of time. Remember, not all dogs need a tie-down. If your dog is practicing socially acceptable behavior in your house, you may never need to use it. We do, however, recommend you acclimate a new puppy to the tie-down system in case you find it is needed at a later date.

Routines Help You Get What You Want

One of the most powerful forms of training that humans can do with dogs is to create routines. The problem is that sometimes the routines you create aren't the ones you want. Sandy learned this the hard way. She had no idea that she was creating a routine she'd later regret when she inadvertently taught her bulldog, Ted, to bark for a treat every time she turned on her hair dryer. The first time Ted barked, probably out of curiosity, when Sandy started drying her hair, she stopped and gave him a cookie to get him to shut up. Sometimes dogs can be very fast learners, and getting a cookie was a communication that Ted understood. As soon as Sandy started to dry her hair, Ted was right there barking until he got a cookie.

Sandy had to laugh when she told this story. It was obvious to her how well-trained *she* had become. She knew breaking the routine would be tougher than starting it, so she decided to do the weaning process in stages. The first few days she gave Ted a treat before turning on the hair dryer. Then she went into the bathroom and shut the door while drying her hair. The next few days she shut the door and ignored his barking while she was drying her hair, but spent some time playing with him as soon as she was finished. She gave him his treat at different times of the day. Within two weeks, Ted had stopped barking every time he heard the hair dryer.

Sandy's new plan took extra time for a week, but it saved her years of stress and annoyance. Ted was a happier dog when he didn't have to experience his mommy's annoyance. And she and Ted created a new and better routine.

You can create more successful communication with your dog by purposefully creating routines and sticking to them. Lynn and Hal's dogs know their morning routine and expect it every day. If something happens out of order, the dogs protest with an extremely soft bark until the offending parent corrects the procedure. The dogs know that first they get their pills, then a treat, then their teeth brushed, then another treat, and only then do they go outside to hang out in their yard until it's time for a walk. They also know that the first quarter mile of the walk is the time for them to sniff every bush and blade of grass before Lynn gets impatient and decides that what the entire family needs, including the dogs, is exercise. They're lucky to get a sidelong look at a bush once Mom is on her mission; although on the days they walk with their dad, Hal, they know they have a different routine: sniffing to their hearts' content.

Setups Eliminate the Last-Resort Punishment

Setups focus on solutions for the future. They are always nonpunitive, and they require a good deal of thinking outside the box. Sometimes they require help from another person to work with you. But it's the advance planning that really defines them. What you need to do is find a way to simulate a situation where your dog can make a mistake and receive a nonpunitive correction that appears to come from his or her behavior and not from you. Sound complicated? It's not as difficult as you might think, especially when you use the Pup Parenting Plan to help you organize for a solution that gets you a step ahead of your pooch while making his behavior less palatable. That's what Jennifer did when her cocker spaniel, Molly, misbehaved around company. Here's how Jennifer used the Pup Parenting Plan.

1. The behavior that bothers me: I want to teach Molly "visitor manners." Molly has a habit of bringing her ball to each guest, dropping it in their lap, and waiting for the person to throw the ball. Telling my friends, "Please do not play with Molly right now because she is manipulating you and being demanding," has no effect. They think Molly is so cute. They can't stop themselves from throwing the ball. Little do they realize that once thrown, the now-slimy ball will be re-dropped in their laps for round two, three, four, and more.

2. Why change is needed: I want my company to enjoy a visit without being nudged, pawed, and jumped on.

3. The mistake I am making: Lacking a plan and following through.

4. A list of possible solutions:

   • Put her in a crate when company comes.

   • Stop having company.

   • Use the tie-down system.

   • Hide all the balls.

   • Ask my company to ignore her.

   • Practice obedience cues.

5. Choose a solution and follow through: Jennifer chose the last two options, but realized she'd have to practice

in advance with someone who had a lot of patience, since most of her friends were either irritated or fascinated by Molly's behavior and would be of no help. She asked her friend Trent to come by to assist with the training. She explained to Trent that they would be practicing a setup by simulating a visit, and it might take several sessions to get Molly to reverse her annoying behavior. She and Trent would agree in advance what they'd do every time Molly brought the ball to him. No matter how he felt, he was to follow the plan.

What Worked for Jennifer and Molly

Trent said he could stop by after work each day for a week so that he and Jennifer could practice. "Trent, you're an angel. Thank you. Okay, here's what we'll do. I want you to walk into the house, greet Molly briefly, and then sit on the couch while I take Molly to her tie-down spot." Jennifer requested that Trent ignore all of her training methods or the mistakes made by Molly and continue carrying on a conversation as if all were fine. Trent said he would be happy to do that.

When he arrived for the first training session, he noticed that Molly was walking around with a short leash attached to her collar. He greeted Molly with his usual scratch behind her ears and then sat down. As if on cue, Molly delivered her ball into his lap, but this time Trent, who had been primed by Jennifer, sat with folded hands as if the ball weren't there. Jennifer picked up Molly's leash, quietly and firmly walked her to the other side of the room and put her in her tie-down place, saying, "We'll try again later." Notice that her method was nonpunitive and delivered in a quiet (and loving) voice. Then she attempted to engage in conversation with Trent, ignoring Molly's barking and whining whenever necessary without saying another word. She also tossed dog treats to Molly to reinforce her when she was quiet as she learned how to behave in her tie-down spot.

When Trent questioned Jennifer's methods, she reassured him that this was important to her and for Molly and that she appreciated his help. Although he looked doubtful, he continued to keep his part of the training bargain. Molly had to be corrected many times the first three days, which isn't unusual, as things often get worse before they get better, but Jennifer persisted. By the fourth day Molly had to be corrected only once. By the fifth day, Molly could greet visitors without insisting they play "slobber catch."

There were times during the training sessions when Trent was concerned that Jennifer was "torturing" poor Molly. He'd ask, "Wouldn't it be kinder to put her in the garage while we visit or when she is pesty?" Jennifer would smile and say, "Been there, done that, and it didn't work." (Many dogs get increasingly worse and more excitable and aggressive when they are isolated in a garage or laundry room while company visits. Not being able to be part of the family increases frustration and often intensifies existing behavior problems.) "I know this is a drag, but we are making progress. We couldn't do this without your help, could we Molly?"

Because Jennifer set up special training times for Molly, she never got to the point of frustration and exhaustion that she might have experienced had she tried to think on the fly. Had she not planned ahead with Trent, she would have been embarrassed and angry with Molly's behavior. She wouldn't have felt comfortable expecting a friend to help unless he had been prompted in advance as to what he was getting into. Despite the inane conversations while they pretended to ignore Molly, Jennifer and Trent actually had a fun time watching the dog's antics. (Remember, this is supposed to be fun.)

> If dogs could talk, what would Molly say? "What's going on here? I thought I had these guys trained to throw my ball, but they seem to be training me. I'm not sure I like this, but if they play catch with me outside later, I'll forgive them."

Setups helped the Kobreys' rottweiler, Kelsey, stop dragging a sock from point A to point B. Since the Kobreys had two young boys, Kelsey was in sock-lying-around heaven. They learned how to use the shaker can setup. They made their own can by putting some pebbles in a soda can (coins would work too) and duct-taping the top to keep the pebbles in the can. They simulated a training situation by making a pile of clothes in the laundry room and stuck a few socks in it so Kelsey could find them. (Kelsey dragged only socks around, and could find a sock anywhere.) As soon as she dove into the pile after a sock, from a hiding spot, they shook the can before her mouth touched a sock. It worked so well, that after a few times, she never grabbed a sock again.

Setups Solve Even Extreme Problems

Pat and John became stepparents to Boo, a ninety-two-pound mix breed that their daughter brought home one day after being away for some time. They never got the complete story about how she found Boo or where he came from, but it didn't take long to realize that Boo had a serious problem—submission urination. Boo peed whenever he met someone who made eye contact with him. After a visit to the vet to make sure his problem wasn't medical, Pat and John were told that the cure was to increase Boo's self-confidence.

Pat took Boo to obedience classes for "neurotic" dogs. He attended advanced obedience training and two agility classes. Boo took to the class immediately and became the best dog in class. His self-confidence soared, but he still peed whenever John came near him. (The theory was that in the past a male head of household probably beat him.)

Although the urination problem got somewhat better, it persisted, so the family members made a plan. First they tried the tie- down method, but it fell flat. The minute John walked in the door, Boo jumped up from his tie-down spot and urinated on everything between him and the end of his tie-down. Next they decided to put Boo on the back deck until John came in and Boo calmed down. The problem with that method was that John had to walk under the deck to get into the house. Yes, Boo peed all over him as he tried to dodge the dog's urine under the deck. Finally the family members agreed to take Boo outside to meet John. John would call on his cell phone from a block away saying that he was almost home, and could they please bring Boo outside. At last they had a method that worked. John would let Boo see him, pee, and then come close so he could greet the dog. After doing this for several weeks, Boo stopped peeing when he saw John.

You can even use a setup to help two dogs in the same household get along. In fact, you can use a setup to help ten dogs in a household get along at mealtime. A doggy day care mother waited patiently till all dogs were sitting before she delivered their food dishes. The minute any dog broke rank, she removed all dishes, waited, and tried again. She said that it took her about fifteen minutes to train the dogs, and the time was well worth the effort. Unless there were several new dogs at day care at one time, the dogs knew and kept to the routine, training newcomers through some soundless, sightless signals they gave each other.

If your dog has the bad habit of eating feces, the shaker can (see page 142) works beautifully. Although we recommend that you keep your dog yard clean, there are times when some dogs will eat their own feces (a condition called coprophagia), and this must be stopped. By finding a hiding spot and waiting for your dog to lean over ready to start eating and then shaking the can, you are creating the perfect setup. Your dog doesn't associate the correction with you, but rather with his behavior. He doesn't like the noise, and he soon figures out that he can control it by not leaning over and eating feces.

When all else fails, you can see how setups help you get a step ahead of your dog and help your dog learn to stop behaviors that are unacceptable. They are worth the time and training, as they prevent more serious measures from being needed. With Molly, a life in the garage was on the horizon. In Boo's case, without the setups, he might have had to be given away or, worse, put down. Day care dogs stealing food from each other could end up with fur flying and blood running, neither being good for the dogs or for business. And the feces-eating dog could become deathly ill. You can make setups work with your dog if you're willing to be proactive, creative, and patient.

If dogs could talk, here's what they'd have to say about setups: "I can't understand why my old behavior is no longer working, but I'm really relieved that my dog mom and dad are showing me how to succeed in the family."

KIND AND FIRM PUP PARENTING PRINCIPLES

1. There is no finish line when it comes to raising kids, whether human or canine.

2. Punishment, shaming, and guilt have no place in pup parenting.

3. When you think of your dog's behavior as normal rather than a personal defiance, you are more likely to succeed in teaching your pup new behaviors.

4. Use an ounce of prevention, a drag lead, a tie-down, routines, or setups to help your dog succeed in the family.

5. Take the time needed for training and give your dog and the problems your full attention. In this way, you won't have to repeat corrections over and over because your dog will stop doing the behaviors that bother you.

CHAPTER 8

PERSONALITY TYPES OF DOGS AND THEIR PEOPLE

"Some day, if I ever get a chance, I shall write a book or warning on the character and temperament of the Dachshund and why he can't be trained and shouldn't be. I would rather train a striped zebra to balance an Indian club than induce a Dachshund to heed my slightest command."

—E. B. White

Any pup parent who has had more than one dog knows that each dog has a unique personality. Still, there are times when you wonder what is normal, what's not normal, and how to deal with your dog's uniqueness in the best ways possible. Factor in your own personality, and the possibilities are endless. Luckily, there are two psychologists coauthoring this book who will be introducing information about personality that has never before been seen in a book about dogs.

Most behaviorists and psychologists debate whether it is nature or nurture that determines how your canine kids (and human ones, too) will behave. We add a twist to the debate. While we would agree that breeds come with predictable behaviors and how you nurture your dog affects their personalities, we add a dose of something you might not be aware of. Your dog makes interpretations (decisions) about what is happening around him, and those interpretations, along with what he was born with (genetics/nature) and how he is parented (nurture), make up his personality.

Here's a case in point. Luisa believes her dog, Scrabble, a five-year-old Airedale, is a "control freak." According to Luisa, Scrabble falls asleep with one foot looped over some part of her body, or he sleeps at her feet so she can't get up without him noticing. Luisa complained that she can't go anywhere without Scrabble knowing. When she does get up, Scrabble wakes up and follows her or watches to make sure she's in view. Luisa has had other Airedales who behaved quite differently, so she's wondering if there might be something wrong with this dog.

Some folks might pathologize Scrabble's behavior, assigning him an "illness" called separation anxiety. Some would say Scrabble's behavior is genetic. Others would look at his personality as a direct result of how he was parented by Luisa, citing her as a person who didn't know how to assert herself as top dog. Then there are those who would remind you that, since an Airedale is known to be a guard dog who can be an opportunist at home, Luisa is simply projecting her interpretation of the dog's behavior onto the dog.

We'd say that this dog's personality is more likely a combination of nature (Airedale qualities) and nurture (Luisa's parenting style), combined with the choices that Scrabble made based on his interpretation of Mom's cues. He reads Luisa's sighs and groans, along with her lack of action, as an invitation that she likes having him at her side. He's also picking up on her need to be needed. Scrabble doesn't have words for all this, but he has enough intuition to hang out a shingle as a psychic.

The Interplay Between Nature, Nurture, and Canine Interpretation

If you're still dubious about personality being formed as part of a process, consider the following. When Lynn brought her new miniature schnauzer, Magic, home on an airplane to join the family, she was small enough to fit in a little carrier under the seat. Her big Samoyed brother, Buddy, was waiting in the car at the airport when Mom came home. Lynn couldn't wait to introduce the two dogs. She opened the car door to pet Buddy while holding Magic in her other hand. Magic took one look at Buddy, put her paw up, leaned into Lynn, and let out a noise that sounded exactly like a human's scream. That wasn't the response Magic's dog mommy had pictured. She was sure the dogs would be instant friends.

As Lynn's husband Hal drove home, Lynn comforted Magic while she and Hal thought up a Plan B for sibling bonding. They decided to look for a park on their way where the two dogs could run freely and get to know each other a bit more slowly. At the park, Mom and Dad agreed to follow a page from Lynn's and Jane's parenting books and allow the two dogs to figure out how to get along, while they kept a close distance if anything should go wrong. They put Magic on the ground and let Buddy off his leash. Other pup parents may have felt protective of the smaller dog, worried that she couldn't hold her own, or thought that the first dog would be jealous of the new dog and want to hurt her. But Lynn and Hal were confident the dogs could sort out their relationship if given an opportunity.

Magic stayed underfoot, while Buddy ran around exploring. Within five minutes, a miracle happened. The two dogs started paying attention to each other, and soon they were romping and playing, with the younger Magic running underneath her new big brother, jumping up and biting his fur. Her brother Bud let her play as roughly as she liked until he had enough. At that point, he gently put his paw on Magic, holding her down until she calmed down. Then, they were off and running again.

This story could have had a different ending if the pup parents had believed that Bud was genetically aggressive or that Magic was genetically fearful when the "scream" happened at the airport. Instead, they put nature and nurture aside in deference to seeing what the dogs would work out on their own. They were close by to intervene if needed, but by watching and waiting, they allowed the dogs to find their unique spots in the family. Buddy became the patient big brother, a personality trait unseen when he had no sibling. Magic became the playful little sister—again, a behavior different from how Lynn saw her interacting with other dogs at the kennel where she found her. Each dog displayed a unique personality that began to emerge through their interaction with each other.

Familiar Models of Canine Classification

Before we introduce you to our system of personality groups, we'll review two well-known methods of canine classification: dividing dogs by function and dividing dogs by breed. Functions include sporting dogs, hounds, working dogs, terriers, toys, non-sporting dogs, herding dogs, and miscellaneous dogs. (Now is a great time to review the table "Dog Groups and Breeds," in Chapter 4 on pages 76–77.) Dividing by breeds often entails as many arguments over what defines a breed as there are breeds. But once categorized, each subdivision has a certain reputation based on stereotypes, as exemplified in the joke that follows.

The question was asked, "How many dogs does it take to change a lightbulb?" Here are the answers, giving you more information than you ever needed on stereotypic breed characteristics.

GOLDEN RETRIEVER: The sun is shining, the day is young, we've got our whole lives ahead of us, and you're inside worrying about a stupid burned-out bulb?

BORDER COLLIE: Just one. And then I'll replace any wiring that's not up to code.

DACHSHUND: You know I can't reach that stupid lamp!

ROTTWEILER: Make me.

BOXER: Who cares? I can still play with my squeaky toys in the dark.

LAB: Oh, me, me!!!!! Pleeeeeeeeeze let me change the lightbulb! Can I? Can I? Huh? Huh? Huh? Can I? Pleeeeeeeeeze, please, please, please!

GERMAN SHEPHERD: I'll change it as soon as I've led these people from the dark, checked to make sure I haven't missed any, and made just one more perimeter patrol to see that no one has tried to take advantage of the situation.

JACK RUSSELL TERRIER: I'll just pop it in while I'm bouncing off the walls and furniture.

OLD ENGLISH SHEEPDOG: Lightbulb? I'm sorry, but I don't see a lightbulb.

COCKER SPANIEL: Why change it? I can still pee on the carpet in the dark.

CHIHUAHUA: Yo quiero Taco Bulb.

POINTER: I see it, there it is, there it is, right there…

GREYHOUND: It isn't moving. Who cares?

AUSTRALIAN SHEPHERD: First, I'll put all the lightbulbs in a little circle…

POODLE: I'll just blow in the border collie's ear and he'll do it. By the time he finishes rewiring the house, my nails will be dry.

Yes, the list is made up of one cliché after another, but if you've parented any of the breeds mentioned, you can almost picture them saying the same thing.

Pup Personality Types New to Dog Literature

While it may be helpful to understand functions and breeds, we'd like you to consider our system for understanding personality because no two people or dogs are exactly alike, and the more you understand about yourself and your pup, the more able you'll be to make good choices affecting the care of your "babies," without jeopardizing your own well being.

Our system for understanding personality takes a grouping of personality traits and lumps them together into four distinct personality "types." Over a thirty-year period, as empirical researchers, we continually discover traits falling into these four groups—both in humans and in canines. The four personality types we've identified are *comfort*, *superiority*, *control*, and *pleasing*. Although you or your dog may have qualities from each group, you'll most likely lead with one of them, especially if you are stressed.

A person or dog with the comfort personality is seeking peace of mind and happiness. The superiority personality has to find meaning and importance in all of his life experiences. The control personality wants to be recognized by being helpful. The pleasing personality just wants to please others while he enjoys whatever he's doing. Each personality type also comes with different baggage, assets, and challenges. Once you identify which personality type your dog has, you'll want to pay special consideration to the needs of that particular kind.

If you haven't already, it's time to figure out what category you're in as well as your dog. How would you answer the following question: What two qualities do you hate to deal with the most— pain and stress, meaninglessness and unimportance, criticism and ridicule, or rejection and hassles? How you answer that question will tell you what personality type you have. If you said pain and stress, you're a comfort pup parent. Think of yourself like the turtle who avoids trouble by pulling into its shell. If meaninglessness and unimportance were your top pick, your personality type is called superiority. You are like the lion, roaring one minute and sleeping the next. For those of you who chose criticism and ridicule, you're in the control group. You're like the eagle, dreaming about flying on the thermals or hiding out by yourself high in your nest. If you chose rejection and hassles, you're a pleasing personality type, like the chameleon who can change colors from one minute to the next to blend in and feel safe.

To find your dog's personality, read more about each personality type until you find the one that most closely matches your dog. This information isn't like a manual for fixing a car; it's not that concrete. But by the time you've read the descriptions of the four personalities and reviewed the charts on pages 156–61, we expect you will be saying, "That's me. There's my dog. No wonder we're having a hard time with such and such. Wow, good thing I didn't get a dog with that personality type!" The charts will assist you in discovering more about your personality and your dog's special needs.

The Comfort (Turtle) Personality

One pup parent with the comfort personality told us, "I've never had a trained dog, just the goal of having a trained dog, and the trainer comes to us, because that's comfortable. My dog gets overweight because I don't want him to be hungry, and I always worry that he'll escape if he gets out. I've always had escape dogs. I'm afraid to give him his freedom to see if he'd go out in front and stick around, so when my dog does get out the front door into forbidden territory, he takes off." When another comfort parent's dog died, she saved his ashes so they can be buried with her when she dies because, she said, her dog didn't like being left alone. Now there's a unique spin on trying to do everything to help others avoid pain and stress—comfort from the grave! Our word of caution for you: Be careful that your efforts to protect don't lead to a helpless dog who "decides" to be fearful of others and becomes too lazy to exercise because he has never had to.

Does your dog have the comfort personality style? Remember the dachshund in the lightbulb joke—the one who couldn't reach the "stupid lamp"? That dachshund wouldn't change the lightbulb even if he had a padded ladder to climb. Why not? Too much work and too stressful. Wendy's dog, Peeky, refused to go on walks. Instead of insisting that Peeky go for even short walks, Wendy puts her in a stroller. Does your dog crave the easy life, like a little peekapoo (or at least the peekapoo's reputation)? Or maybe your dog is like a basset hound, a calm pet that enjoys and needs human companionship, but can become extremely stubborn if spoiled. If so, chances are your dog has the comfort style.

Lynn's miniature schnauzer fits the bill for the comfort personality because she's a therapy dog who brings comfort to others. She also loves her pillows (lots of them) and her cuddle time and just tolerates her walks. When she gets hot or tired, she plunks her small but compact body down in the middle of the path and refuses to move until carried. She'd prefer to pee in the house than to go outside in the rain or wind, and has no use for her yellow rain slicker because it's too uncomfortable!

Do the descriptions of comfort fit you or your dog? Use the chart on page 158 to help you learn more about yourself and/or your pup.

The Superiority (Lion) Personality

If you'd most like to avoid meaninglessness and unimportance, you have a superiority personality style. You have a lot of drive, intensity, and focus and can get things done. If you fall into this category, you're extremely knowledgeable, but you probably suffer from the insecurity that there is always a little bit more to learn, a little bit more to do, another class to take, and just one more try to be perfect. Yes, you're a perfectionist who runs on shoulds, musts, and have tos. You hate wasting your time on anything that isn't meaningful to you. You like to be "right" and appreciated. You'd probably get a whole lot more appreciation and acquiescence if you stopped roaring like a lion and started listening to others—which you can be very good at.

You want to be sure you have the right dog for a meaningful relationship. A purebred dog might be best, from championship stock if at all possible—unless you decide that the right thing to do is to adopt. Then your focus might shift from winning ribbons to saving the world. You have a lot of social consciousness. Superiority parents are often seen by others as scary and attacking like a big old lion. But when they look in the mirror, all they see is a sweet little pussycat who has just coughed up a hair ball to clean out their system. Yes, you tend to get over whatever is bothering you once you express it, even if those around you might need a lot more time to lick their wounds.

Are you this kind of pup parent? If so, do you look for someone to tell you the right way to treat your dog and then do it without question? Or are you indecisive—always looking for more information? Does the sign on your desk say, "Don't bother to agree with me. I've already changed my mind"? We know you always want to do what's best for your dog—at least, what you believe is best. You probably don't realize that you operate on a lot of assumptions, so it would be helpful to check them before proceeding. Our advice to you—relax. You have nothing to prove to be loved and admired. Your dog loves you. Don't forget, there are lots of "right ways" to parent a pooch.

What kind of dog comes to mind when you think about the superiority/lion personality type? Think back to the greyhound from the lightbulb joke; that was the dog who said, "If it isn't moving, who cares?" It would be a waste of his time to do something that he didn't find important. Or, take one look at an Afghan, sometimes called the "King of Dogs," with the aloof look and aristocratic bearing. He's the perfect stereotype for this personality type. Samoyeds also come to mind, as they don't like to do anything that isn't meaningful to them. They have been known to fetch a ball once to show you that they know how, but if you throw it again, they'd prefer that you get it yourself. How about the highly intelligent, noble collie who, at least in the movies, can save the day when all others fail? Or the French poodle, a highly intelligent, easy to train, elegant, chi-chi dog. The superiority/lion dog would be the dog (please note that the word *pooch* is highly unappealing to this personality type) who is well bred, intelligent, perfectionistic, and used to being top dog.

The Control (Eagle) Personality

If you want to avoid criticism and ridicule, the control personality type is you. You like to cover all your bases in advance to prevent any possible problems from happening. You're not crazy about delegating, as no one can do a job as well as you can. You ignore your feelings and have an amazing ability to engage in difficult physical pursuits because you can bypass pain. Of course, you often end up injured or sick because you don't listen to the signals your body is trying to send you. You may feel lonely because you isolate and hold back, but when given time and space to work things out by yourself, you're ready to try again. You appreciate a good listener and have an intense need to have choices. You're the world's procrastinator and pile person, trying to convince yourself (and others) that you can put your hand on any piece of paper in your pile at a moment's notice if you only had the time to look. You're a service-oriented person who likes to help others and focus on them, often at your own expense.

Since you don't realize that it's okay to do what you want (and that this won't make you selfish), you tend to take care of everyone else's needs and spin in circles trying to cover for every last problem that might go wrong.

What are the dogs that come to mind with this same control personality type? The rottweiler and border collie from the lightbulb joke fit the bill, as does the St. Bernard, complete with brandy flask, ignoring physical pain to rescue the poor guy lost in the snow. Or the English sheepdog or Australian shepherd, herding the flock, working to keep everything under control. How about the German shepherd, helping the police, catching the bad guys, sniffing out drugs, and generally looking like a guard dog no one would want to mess with. Or what about the Doberman or pit bull, two dogs who have a reputation for being tough.

Sparky, a tan-and-white cocker spaniel, a dog you wouldn't normally associate with this personality group, is a great example of the control dog. He figured out that his Mom was deaf in one ear. Through trial and error, he learned to "get" Mom and lead her to another room where she was needed, by yipping and prancing at her feet and making eye contact. Then he'd head toward another room, always checking that Mom would follow him. He saved Mom from several pots boiling over and alerted her to the doorbell ringing. Sparky had never been trained to do this. He just figured it out on his own. He saw the need to jump in and cover the bases so that the family could be safe, and he took charge.

The Pleasing (Chameleon) Personality

Do you most want to avoid rejection and hassles? That puts you in the pleasing personality group, smack dab in the middle of the pup parents who say yes when they mean no, want everyone to get along, love harmony and hate confrontations, and insist that they'd hurt someone's feelings if they told the truth (although we're sure they are really more concerned about staying in everyone's good graces). They can change their personality to fit any situation they are in (like the chameleon that represents this style), which makes them sensitive and accommodating and observant and intuitive. They are friendly and flexible, but if you hurt their feelings, which is easy to do because they are thin-skinned, they'll probably tell ten other people before they tell you. Their life would be better if they said what they thought and made sure they had plenty of alone time each day to regroup. It wouldn't hurt them to practice saying no every day, either, without explaining themselves for hours.

Several dogs come to mind when thinking about this personality type. First are the golden retriever, black Labrador, and cocker spaniel, who seem to live to please their family members. They also seem to have an insatiable need to be petted and have a lot of undivided attention from their parents. To others, they could appear to be spoiled and pesky; to you they are your loves. They are the dogs that jog at your side without a leash and come when called, every time.

The other kind of dog that comes to mind is more a type of dog than a particular breed. We call them the "purse" dogs because they rarely walk and are most often carried from place to place. Remember Reese Witherspoon's Chihuahua in the *Legally Blonde* films? These dogs usually have a bigger wardrobe than the rest of the family, including matching jewelry and carrying bags. Their parents talk to them in baby talk and call them funny names, like "my little mush-mush," or "sweetie-tweety-pie." If a stranger gets near them, they growl ferociously until their parents pet them and whisper words of comfort like, "Was that mean old person trying to scare you? Shame on them!" You've got the picture. They are a princess or prince in dog's clothing.

(continued on page 162)

Personality Style	Wants	Pays the Price of:	Assets	
PUP PARENT PERSONALITY PROFILE				
Personality Style	**Wants**	**Pays the Price of:**	**Assets**	
Comfort/Turtle Pup Parent	To experience the easy life	Boredom, procrastination, lack of productivity, loneliness, avoiding new experiences, lots of physical problems	Going with the flow, able to express your feelings, supportive, helpful, reliable, persistent, fun-loving, creative	
Superiority/Lion Pup Parent	To find meaning and importance in life	Feeling exhausted, over-burdened, imperfect	Creative, idealistic, self-starter, independent, capable, clear about what is important	
Control/Eagle Pup Parent	To be helpful and involved	Lack of intimacy and spontaneity, doing everything yourself, procrastination, physical problems, defensiveness, inflexibility, needing permission before acting, catastrophizing	A great crisis manager, patient, persevering, loyal, helpful, objective, willing to do what other people won't	
Pleasing/ Chameleon Pup Parent	To enjoy whatever you do	Not knowing who you are, overly apologetic, too agreeable, easily hurt, harboring resentment, feeling overlooked, being overly sensitive to other people's energy, being misunderstood, and getting rejected	Accepting, open-minded, adaptable, genuinely interested in others, good listener, optimistic, empathetic, generous, fun-loving	

	Challenges	Best Dog Personality Match for You
	Your dog will never lack for cuddling, but don't forget to exercise your dog. Use a leash when walking, pick up after your dog, and make sure your dog is obedience-trained. Everyone isn't as crazy about your dog as you are, so don't inflict your dog on others.	Superiority dogs will be too demanding for you. You'd do best with comfort, control, or pleasing dogs.
	Remember there are shades of gray. Be curious, explore different points of view rather than clinging to the notion that there is one right way and it's yours. Check things out and have the courage to be imperfect. Learn to be satisfied with your efforts and your dog's efforts. Since you can go from one extreme to another, there may be times that your dog will be a lower priority and miss out on the great care you are able to give.	Comfort dogs will bore you and pleasing dogs may end up annoying you after awhile. You'd do best with superiority dogs and control dogs.
	Listen to your feelings, do what you want, delegate, and finish what you start. Give yourself a break and stop worrying about your dog. Your constant vigilance can drive your dog (and others) nuts. You are a great crisis manager, but you may need to follow a schedule or make a list so you don't miss those dry water bowls or empty bags of dog food. Slow down and follow through on the logistics of life.	You'd enjoy a comfort dog who is happy with all you can do for her, a superiority dog who demands a lot from you, and a pleasing dog who shows you a lot of love. Be careful with a control dog so you don't get into a power struggle over who is boss.
	Learn to say no and ask for help so you don't resent your pup. You are probably worrying too much about your dog's happiness. Trust that your dog is fine. You're overly sensitive, so let some things go. If you think it, say it without malice or anger. These behaviors will reduce your anxiety so you can enjoy pup parenting more.	You can adapt to any kind of dog, so choose the dog that pleases you most. However, since you might not be good at getting the most out of your dog during obedience training, pick a dog that follows commands and is easier to train. Chances are you will have many different kinds of dogs over the years with all the personalities.

PUP PERSONALITY PROFILE				
Personality Style	Care and Feeding of a Dog with this Personality	If Dogs Could Talk	Avoid Pup Parents Who	
Comfort/Turtle Dog	Don't overpet or overindulge us. If you feel sorry for us and make exceptions to the general care that all dogs need, we can end up with a lot of physical problems, including obesity. *Do not* let us run the house because it won't be good for either of us. If you haven't noticed, we can be very stubborn, so we need you to do what's best for us, like keeping us on a routine and making sure we go outside regularly to do our business.	Is there anything bigger than a king-size bed? If not, would you mind sleeping on the couch? I know you think I should be able to curl up in a ball like a cat, but I'm so much happier perpendicular, with my tail sticking out in one direction and my front paws in the other.	We can bring out the worst in any pup parent. If you have a superiority personality and get too demanding, we'll balk. If you have a control personality, we'll let you be boss just so long, and then we'll balk. If you have a pleasing personality, we'll be happy as long as you constantly try to please us; when you stop, we'll balk. And if you have a comfort personality, we worry that you won't take care of us.	

Personality Style	Care and Feeding of a Dog with this Personality	If Dogs Could Talk	Avoid Pup Parents Who
Superiority/Lion Dog	We are never going to be happy without a challenge or a chance to do what is meaningful to us. We like new places and adventures. We also like having a job. It's important to us to look good and be well cared for. Don't expect us to always do what you want, because if the request isn't important to us, we won't do it. Do *not* get into a power struggle with us because you will either lose or break our spirit. More than you realize, we often know what's best for us, so consider following our lead.	Of course we can understand verbal instructions, hand signals, whistles, horns, clickers, beepers, scent IDs, electromagnetic energy fields, and Frisbee flight paths. But it's a good thing we love you so much or we wouldn't respond to any of them.	We are never going to be happy with a pup parent who doesn't challenge us, so comfort parents may not be best for us. Superiority parents can be a bit too perfectionistic and hard-driving, but we'll do our best to keep up. If pleasing parents follow our lead, we're fine. We love control parents who realize what is meaningful to us and then work hard to make sure we get what we want and need.

PUP PERSONALITY PROFILE

Personality Style	Care and Feeding of a Dog with this Personality	If Dogs Could Talk	Avoid Pup Parents Who	
Control/Eagle Dog	We thrive on routines— routines for eating, walking, playing, training, eliminating, grooming. We need a hobby or a job or a way to help you. We love Shutzhund training, obedience classes, helping you introduce new dogs to the family, herding farm animals, watching the baby, guarding the house. We also need lots of physical activity. We will run by your side with great joy, or chase a ball or Frisbee for hours. We'll retrieve your ducks if you're a hunter, running through thick and thin to please you, but we need lots of "atta boys." Never use punishment with us; it's unnecessary and invites bigger problems.	Under this tough exterior beats a heart of gold. Just don't cross our line, though, because we can't guarantee what will happen if our heart turns from gold to cold. If you see our ears go back, our tails go down, and our lip curl, we suggest you do a quick disappearing act till we calm down.	We can be slow learners, so if you have overly high expectations, forget about us. Superiority pup parents will have to learn patience. Pleasing parents will have to realize that we don't really care if we please others, but we want to please you. Comfort parents are probably not a match for us, as we require a lot of work.	

Personality Style	Care and Feeding of a Dog with this Personality	If Dogs Could Talk	Avoid Pup Parents Who
Pleasing/ Chameleon Dog	Since we will do just about anything within our power to please you, be careful what you wish for. Don't overtax us and don't, don't, don't overreward us for obnoxious behavior because you'll never see the end of it. We are so easy to train that you never need to use harsh methods. A quick jerk on a collar is about all it takes to get us walking at your side. Do give us lots of opportunities to show love with children, friends, neighbors, and other family members. And make sure you do things that please us, too. The Labs will love hanging out around water; the goldens will enjoy their romps at the dog park, getting a chance to say hello to other dogs; and the purse dogs will appreciate a cute little bow from the groomer.	When we get to the Pearly Gates, do we have to shake hands to get in? It gets so tiresome trying to be nice all the time. And by the way, I like smelling the other dog's butts before I kiss you, and it's about time you found this cute and adorable.	We are quite sensitive, so if a lot of grooming isn't your thing, or if you have allergies, we won't be happy, because you won't be pleased with us. We will follow your commands and learn quickly. If you want a free-spirit dog, that's not us. Comfort parents make us very happy, as do control parents who want to look out for us. But we don't like it if you are too overprotective. Superiority parents need not apply unless you think we are totally superior just the way we are.

Cindy Adams's dog, Jazzy (a Yorkshire terrier), fits the bill for the pleasing/chameleon personality type. She's a little diva, with a driver who picks her up from doggy play dates and a bevy of dog walkers who help Mommy out. Then there is Brie, the two-year-old, twenty-pound French bulldog who has become a gold mine to her parents. Not only do they love her, but enough people love her that she has her own talent agent. According to the *San Francisco Chronicle*, she has a greeting card line, and soon might be her parent's retirement plan if she gets "discovered" at the international licensing show, where she could become the "next big thing." In the meantime, Brie loves to get her nails done and wear her new faux Tahitian pearl necklace.

A little pug named Bounce also fits the pleasing/chameleon bill. Bounce is kind of a screwball, according to his Mom. He does something she's read about in pug books that she calls "happy dancing" or "crazy dog." He takes off and runs around in circles at ninety miles an hour with his tail straight out. Mom asks, "How could a dog who makes everyone laugh have anything but a pleasing personality?"

As a pup parent, the pleasing/chameleon is always worried if her babies are happy, although she'd gladly delegate whatever jobs are needed to accomplish that. Are you like that? Do you have (or would you like to have) a dog walker to play with your dog? A dog sitter to watch your dog while you're off on some grand adventure? A dog groomer to brush your dog? A sherpa of your choice to make sure your dog gets to the vet, gets her pills, gets her food, and so forth? If this is your personality style, we highly recommend you stop worrying about whether your dog is happy, stop running in circles trying to please everyone, and sit still long enough to pet, snuggle, or play with your pooch.

Now What?

Did you find yourself nodding your head or smiling when you read about one of the types? Could you see yourself or your dog doing some of the behaviors found in each group? Keep your eyes open as you interact with your pooch or watch others do the same, and soon you may be seeing turtles, lions, eagles, and chameleons everywhere.

We've noticed that the personality type behaviors get more extreme when you or your dog are stressed. In these times, your behaviors are so reactive and automatic, they serve as a barrier to doing what is needed in the situation. The turtle hides in his shell, the lion roars and attacks, the eagle backs off and flies in circles, going nowhere, and the chameleon is like a deer frozen in the headlights. When you are in your most extreme behavior, protecting instead of moving forward with grace and joy, you might want to ask yourself, "What am I afraid of? What's the worst thing that could happen? Could I handle it?" Amazingly, asking those questions often calms you down and helps you move forward.

Tips on Using Personality Information

Here's another suggestion for dealing with yourself or your pup when behavior seems edgy and cranky. Try out one or more of the tips below.

1. Since there are four different personality styles, don't take behaviors personally. They are more likely a sign of a personality difference than a personal affront.

2. Cut yourself (and your dog) some slack and be more accepting of unique wants and needs.

3. If you are stressed, give yourself the following:

    -   *Comfort:* Any small step will do; believe in yourself

    -   *Superiority:* Space, relaxation, patience, and a pat on your back for progress

    -   *Control:* Permission to do what you want and time to think things through

    -   *Pleasing:* Ask someone for help, set boundaries, find an expert you respect and take their advice

4. If your dog is stressed, she may need the following:

- *Comfort:* Shorter walks, softer pillows, extra pets

- *Superiority:* Trust in his ability, a place to show off, do what he likes most

- *Control:* Give her a job, let her accompany you whenever possible, show her a lot of love

- *Pleasing:* Tell her how adorable she is, have plenty of his favorite snacks and toys on hand, and dress her cute

KIND AND FIRM PUP PARENTING PRINCIPLES

1. Your dog's personality is a mix of nature, nurture, and your dog's interpretations of what happens.

2. Anyone who has had more than one dog in a particular breed knows that breed stereotypes only go so far, because personality differences are normal within breeds. You could have dogs from each personality type within the same breed.

3. You and your dog each have a personality style, which greatly affects your relationship.

4. The more you are aware of differences within personality styles, the more you will understand what is best for you and your pup.

5. Different personalities require different kinds of encouragement. Make sure you give the specific encouragement that is needed.

CHAPTER 9

IT TAKES A VILLAGE
TO RAISE A DOG

"On the first day of creation, God created the dog.

On the second day, God created man to serve the dog.

On the third, God created all the animals of the earth to serve as potential friends for the dog.

On the fourth day, God created honest toil so that man could labor for the good of the dog.

On the fifth day, God created the tennis ball so that the dog might or might not retrieve it.

On the sixth day, God created veterinary science to keep the dog healthy and the man broke.

On the seventh day, God tried to rest, but He had to walk the dog."

With the opening anecdote, we don't mean to make light of creation or religion. We're simply making a point, with the help of author unknown, just how much work it is to parent a dog. We think Hillary Clinton had the right idea when she penned the title to her book, It Takes a Village.

Although Mrs. Clinton was referring to human children, those of us who are pooch parents have discovered that it also takes a community effort to raise Fido. Whether you are a working or stay-at-home parent, you've already figured out that you need help from others.

A pet store for food and supplies was probably your first contact outside the family to help you care for your dog. Then came the veterinarian. Possibly, the groomer was the next person you added to your list. After that, did you find a need for day care? Pet sitters? Kennels? Carpet cleaners? Dog bakeries? Behaviorists? Obedience classes? Photographers? Internet buddies and advice givers? Psychics? Animal psychiatrists? Dog-friendly hotels? Restaurants? Dog parks? Camps? Chiropractors? Alternative healers? Foster parents? Portrait painters? Show handlers? And yes, even plastic surgeons?

As extravagant as the roles of these people might be, let us not forget that parenting a pooch may also involve coparents, children, grandparents, other relatives, and friends. Then there's the boy- or girlfriend who announces, "If you want me, you get the dog!" (Or the true compatibility test from the soon-to-be-ex potential mate who says, "If you want me, get rid of the dog.") It's a family affair to parent a pooch. Given the complexities of relationships, there are many issues that you, as a pup parent, need to address. Our focus in this chapter is on inconsistencies in parenting styles, doggy day care, overnight care, and traveling with Rover. We'll leave the rest in your capable hands.

If Everyone Agreed, You'd Be Living in a Dream

Pup parents, like parents of human children, think they must always agree and provide a united front. We have news for you. Most dogs handle inconsistencies as well as most children do. They quickly figure out who does what, who allows them to get away with something, and who holds them accountable. Then they adjust their behavior accordingly.

Many parents disagree and have not-so-subtle ways of letting each other know. Instead of talking to each other, they talk to the dog: "Did your Mommy let you get away with that?" "Did your Daddy forget to feed you?" Canine kids will survive these inconsistencies just fine, but the couple may need to work on their communication skills to ensure *their* survival.

There are more extreme inconsistencies, however, that can result in horrible chaos from time to time, and they can take a toll on everyone. When dogs are overwhelmed by the chaos in a family, they can easily end up behaving in ways that result in them being unloved and/or unwanted, and it really isn't their fault. This was the case with the Randalls' beagle, Bandit. (One wonders what came first, the name Bandit or his outlaw behavior.)

Ronnie Randall described her family as scattered, running in all different directions with no structure to their life. They had two school-age kids, and everyone in the family dealt with Bandit, the puppy, in their own way, without communicating or consulting each other. Ronnie realized this was at the root of many of their problems, but she was unwilling to use any methods that impaired Bandit's love of freedom. All she wanted to do was to help him break some of his bad habits. "Couldn't someone simply teach Bandit how to hold a sit stay for those times that they needed him to be still?" Considering that Bandit had free rein to do pretty much whatever he pleased, that he had learned to ignore everybody because he didn't understand what anybody wanted from him, that he made up his own rules that made sense to him, and that he was a beagle—a dog notoriously difficult to train in certain areas—the answer was a resounding NO!

Since the Randalls were unwilling to use a crate, a tie-down, or a fenced-in area, their desires were unrealistic. Ronnie was aware of that, but she still hoped for a miracle. She grasped that it would be ridiculous to give cues that no one could enforce. She knew she was potentially putting Bandit's life in danger should he run out the gate and get into traffic, or worse yet, chase sheep on the nearby property and get shot by a farmer. She experienced that a beagle will ignore a request to sit if there is a strong scent on the ground to follow. Yet her parenting style was to love everyone and allow her kids freedom to "raise themselves," and this included her dog.

Ronnie finally agreed to use a cable attached to a tree (see Chapter 4 for more information) so family members could walk through their gate, tie Bandit up on the cable, drive the car in, close the gate, and then let Bandit loose. She used the system when it was convenient, which was about one out of every four trips to and from the garage. The rest of the time, she and the other family members smacked Bandit, yelled at him, or let him run out the gate while they crossed their fingers. Where Bandit is today, no one knows, including the Randalls. But while he lived with the family, he certainly had his freedom.

Inconsistencies Created by Visitors

There are times that the inconsistencies you worry about are the ones created when you have company. Have you had to deal with a few people like a brother, uncle, or best friend who insist on coming in and reinforcing all the behaviors you're trying to stop, like jumping up, rough-and-tumble play, tug-of-war, and other games that will make your dog extremely excited and make him forget his manners? Some dogs with outgoing, gregarious personalities will try these behaviors with everyone who comes through the door.

It's perfectly appropriate for you to inform folks who visit you regularly how you would like them to interact with your dog. It's your home and you have the right to set the standard in your house. You can also put Trixie in a crate, use a tie-down, or "umbilical cord" her to your leg when company comes so that you get to decide who your dog meets and when. If you have a visitor who is uncomfortable around dogs, you can keep your dog on a leash and let your pup interact with folks who want to meet your dog, thus avoiding intimidating dog-fearing guests.

On the other hand, your pooch might be the kind who can play wild with one person without getting too riled up once the party is over. There are those guests who love dogs and enjoy rolling around on the floor with them, throwing a ball a hundred times, and playing with every toy in your dog's toy basket. If this doesn't create bigger problems, take advantage of your good fortune and let your dog have a party! Many dogs can recognize the difference between folks who like to play this way and those who don't, and behave accordingly. An added benefit is that rather than becoming overexcited, she may become exhausted and calm after such a play session.

Hints for Avoiding Inconsistencies with Outside Care

It's irritating when inconsistencies make extra work for you. Have you ever left your baby (human or canine) with a relative or friend while you went on a vacation, only to come back and have to spend a week or more getting your little one back on track? Has this ever happened when you left your pooch at day care or with a dog sitter?

Since so many of you reading this book are working parents who use doggy day care or pet sitters, or are parents who don't take your dogs on vacation with you, we'd like to offer three hints that can help keep things a bit more consistent (and safe) for you and your pooch: (1) make sure the place where you are leaving your pup is set up for your canine's safety; (2) instead of sending written instructions, send a letter from your dog; and (3) take time to introduce your dog to the substitute parent while you're around to ease everyone into the change.

Following our hints can help you avoid learning the hard way, like Samuel and Leona did. They were newlyweds and first-time pup parents. After being turned down by their friends and family members to care for their shar-pei, Escrow, while they honeymooned, they turned to the local phone book. There, they researched extensively to find the best possible care for their dog. Samuel visited many kennels, but he wasn't happy leaving his dog in a caged-in area that to him seemed small, wet, and musty-smelling, and filled with overanxious dogs who had no place to run or exercise. Some places were indoors only, where the dogs had to potty on turf or mats. To Samuel and Leona, these places were dog jails.

They went back to the phone book where they noticed a category called "pet sitting service," a business that employs certified and bonded people to stop by the house to feed and water pets while you are away. The woman they spoke with said walks were optional for a small fee, and that in addition to caring for Escrow, the pet sitter could also feed their fish, water their plants, and pick up the mail. After meeting the owner of the pet sitting service, and asking a lot more questions, Samuel and Leona decided to give it a try. It seemed safe and affordable, and they thought Escrow would be happiest staying in his own house.

When Sam and Leona arrived home from vacation, Escrow was missing. A simple note from their sitter apologizing for his disappearance was left on their dining room table. They called the business office only to discover that the company took no responsibility for the loss, nor apologized for failing to notify them while they were away. Samuel was shocked and Leona was inconsolable. Samuel went searching for Escrow. He started with the closest pound (which was closed for the day) and walked around the perimeter of the fences. He was sure he could hear his dog's bark. Sure enough, he could see his shar-pei in one of the kennels.

Never in their wildest imaginations would Sam and Leona have predicted such a disaster. Had they spoken with us, we would have recommended hiring someone who comes with recommendations from friends or family who have used their service. We'd also recommend a pet sitter who stays at your home while you are away instead of "stopping by."

We are sure that had they looked harder, Sam and Leona, like you, could find a kennel that would be an excellent and safe place to board your dog—one that does not seem like a dog jail. If you can't get a personal recommendation, visit the place and ask the following questions:

- Is there a vet on the premises?

- How many dogs are assigned per staff member?

- Do they sleep indoors or outdoors?

- What is the exercise schedule?

- How long have they been in business?

- Are their certifications and licensing up to date?

- How often are the dogs fed?

- How often are the cages cleaned?

- Are they insured or bonded?

- Do they require all dogs to be vaccinated?

A good boarding kennel has secure fencing, and the risk of the dog getting out is minimal. Of course, it is your responsibility to inform the boarding kennel if your dog is an escape artist so they can put the dog in an escape-proof kennel.

Inspect the boarding kennel to make sure it is clean, safe, has an enclosed exercise area for long-term boarders, and that the proper vaccinations are required. Does it smell good? Will the staff give your dog any necessary medication? Are you allowed to leave some of your dog's favorite toys, treats, and his blanket, or an old shirt of yours? Many people are worried that their dog will be scared, bored, or upset by spending time in a small kennel. Therry was a kennel operator for many years, and she found that this is not what usually happens. The great majority of dogs that stayed in her kennel enjoyed the stay because of the excitement it provided. They got lots of exercise and were well cared for.

Joan visited four different boarding kennels with her poodle, Teddi, before settling on just the right one. What made the difference? All the dogs that were at the kennel on the day Joan visited seemed happy to be there. The forty or so dogs all came around to the front of their area to see if Joan might have come for them, but immediately returned to their previous activity (bone chewing, napping, or playing with kennel mates) when they saw that she wasn't their human. Teddi's many experiences there afterward were all excellent, and Joan's peace of mind when she went away was assured.

You might want to start boarding your dog as a puppy so that she gets accustomed to being away from home. Don't forget to bring some toys and a blanket, and especially your own food so there will be no change of diet during the kennel stay. Make sure you include written instructions, preferably in letter form (examples to follow). If you want your dog to stay at home, as we've already mentioned, pick a house sitter who is a close friend or relative or hire a professional with a good reputation who comes with personal references. It is important that you can trust this person implicitly and know they will stick to your rules and not disrupt the dog's schedule too much and will also take good care of your home as well as your dog. Start with a small step, possibly having the person come the first time while you are home, and then work up to a one-nighter. When you feel comfortable with the person, you can add nights away.

If you use a dog walker, ask for referrals or references and make sure they use your training equipment. Do inform them about your dog's personality traits and habits. If you use a day care program, you need to find out how they go about separating dogs that may not be compatible so as not to endanger small dogs and older dogs that can get hurt by rough play or dogs with a strong predatory instinct. Of course, fencing is everything and vaccinations must be required. You should also check on how the day care deals with flea control.

All of what we've mentioned so far are prerequisites for any outside care to meet. But is it necessary to leave your pooch in a place that has a swimming pool and an endless supply of tennis balls and an on-site doggy therapist? Do you need to leave your babies in the Presidential Suite so that both of your dogs can stay together and you have the choice of paying extra for more play breaks, walks, and grooming? Is it worth paying more for your dogs than you pay for your own hotel room if it gives you peace of mind? We don't think any of these are necessary, but we know that you may feel better leaving your pup at such a place, and they are available in many communities.

Does your dog need "doggy rehab" rather than simple day care? Some pup parents look to doggy day care with that idea in mind. They want their dogs to be better socialized and more fulfilled, and have a second family, not to mention a place that will even housebreak their pup for them. To be eligible, your canine kid may have to pass a test as much as you'll have to approve of the facility. Most places will want to make sure your dog is spayed or neutered, has up-to-date vaccinations, doesn't bite, is in good health, doesn't have fleas or contagious diseases, and most of all, gets along with other dogs.

Have Your Dog Write a Letter to the Substitute Parent

If you give verbal instructions to your substitute parent, they may be forgotten. Leave written instructions instead, and do a "walk through" at your home before you leave for your first overnight. We suggest leaving written instructions in the form of a letter from your dog. They are fun to write and entertaining to read, and give the caregiver a taste of your dog's personality that a dry list of instructions can't convey. Lynn has sent letters to dog sitters from both her dogs. These examples may give you ideas for a letter about your dog.

The first is from Magic (a miniature schnauzer), who stayed with a family for the first time, because they wanted to find out if they'd enjoy having a dog. The letter is a bit lengthy, because though this family had spent time petting Magic and taking her for walks, they had never had a dog stay overnight before. They found the letter extremely helpful and have gone on to invite Magic to stay whenever Lynn and Hal travel. The second letter is from Lynn's twelve-year-old Samoyed, Buddy, to a new dog sitter. Notice that the letter has information about the vet, medication, walks, sleeping arrangements, food, and personality.

Dear Ones,

I'm so excited that I can spend some time at your house. I love new adventures and being with people who think I'm adorable. I'm also looking forward to learning how to speak my native tongue, German. I may look small, but I can hike, play in the snow, and make you feel better when you're sad. I'm ten years old, and if I do say so myself, I think I look quite good for my age, even though I have a large fatty tumor on my chest. The vet says it's my pillow and that I'm used to it. I guess that's okay.

My mom says I'm easy, but what does she know. If you don't pay attention when we are walking, I'll eat anything I can find. I especially like duck poop and grass clippings, even though my mom tries to stop me from eating them. I'm happy when I can sit on the couch, but I won't jump up there (when you are looking) unless you say it's okay. If you're not around, I'll make myself quite comfortable on the softest chair or couch I can find. I love going for rides in the car and have spent many a pleasant afternoon and evening sleeping in the car while my parents go to the movies or out to eat. My favorite stop is the bakery, where my mom gives me a hunk of fresh bread. I really don't like the heat, so please don't leave me in a hot car. But I can stay in the car when it's cold, especially if you bring a bowl of water along.

In case you need to take me to the vet, which I hardly ever go to except for my annual checkups, you can call ... Veterinary Hospital and ask for Dr. ... Her number is ... All my shots are up to date. You have Mom and Dad's permission to take me to the doctor if I need it.

My parents never brush me, so you don't have to do that. I get a bath and cut at the groomers every five weeks, but if I smell and you want to, you can wash me off in the sink or a tub. I love my walks. I'm used to walking in the morning, once during the day, and at night before bed. If you put me out in the yard to go to the bathroom, I might, but I might also forget because I get preoccupied with new smells. But when I'm on my walk, I know it's time to go to the bathroom. Please clean up after me with a plastic bag, and keep me on my leash so I don't eat things that are bad for me that I simply can't resist.

When I walk with someone new, I like to be the boss. I stop all the time because I can. So if I'm being obnoxious, make my leash shorter and keep walking, and I'll get the idea and walk with you. Beware of my famous "hockey stop," which I'm very good at. I put my front feet together, squat, and stop on a dime. When I do that, even a large person has to stop with me. My mom isn't impressed by my fast stop. She simply keeps walking, so I have to do the same. But my dad stops every time I do.

Once I had to have a tooth pulled, so my vet told Mom and Dad (that's what we call Lynn and Hal) to brush my teeth every morning and then give me some special dog treats. It really doesn't do any good, but I love the taste of the toothpaste and the treats, so please remember or I'll be sad. I also have to have a thyroid pill every morning. My mom sticks it in some food so I accidentally eat it while I wolf down the food.

You can put some food in my dish and leave it there and I'll eat it when I'm hungry. Now if you have any cat food around, I prefer that, even though I know it isn't good for me. Sometimes I push my dish around with my nose and try to bury it under a rug or cover it with a pillow. People think I'm weird, but they humor me and let me think I'm a real dog burying my food. I am happy to help you clean your house while I visit. You'll find I'm an excellent vacuum cleaner, eating anything you drop on the floor.

I would love it if I could sleep on a pillow by your bed. My mom can send my leopard pillow with me. If you want me to, I'd be happy to sleep in your bed, but I don't do that unless you invite me up.

(Information about the trip is included in this paragraph, with contact numbers in case of emergency.)

Well, I think that's about it. I like getting petted, but if I am being pesty, just ignore me and I'll settle right down. Licks and cuddles from me and thank-yous from Lynn and Hal,

Magic

Hi there,

Let's start with the important stuff that older people and elderly dogs always lead with: our illnesses, aches, and pains. As you've probably noticed, I have arthritis in my hind legs. I'm on medication for it that I take once a day in the morning. You'll also notice how dirty my right ear is. That's because I have to have drops every day, and they leave a terrible mess. In case I get worse, my vet is...and her number is ... She's at the ... Animal Clinic.

Just because I'm old doesn't mean I don't still enjoy the finer things in life. I love to stay outside most of the day and all of the night. I might hang out with you inside during the day for a little while, but as I've gotten older, I'm much happier in the yard. I love my three walks a day, though. That would be my favorite way of spending time with you. My dad thinks I have to go really slow cuz I'm old, but when my mom has the leash, we go at a pretty good clip. She shows no mercy, although I have noticed that she's cut down our walk from three miles to a little over two miles. Fortunately, she's only around three days a week, so I get a break in between. If you let me, I'll lift my leg on every bush and flower, just so they can say, "Buddy was here!"

If you find writing a letter too tedious and would prefer to leave a simple list, make sure it contains information about the food your dog eats and how often to serve it, any medications your dog needs, the name and number of an emergency contact in addition to the veterinarian, an up-to-date shot record (a must at any reputable kennel), your dog's behavioral history, and your itinerary and contact numbers. Do leave out your dog's favorite pillow or toy (and always bring these to the kennel), and make your good-bye as nonemotional as possible, telling your dog calmly that you are going on a trip, and that you'll be back soon.

I love getting my teeth brushed in the morning. The vet says I have great teeth, and I'm trying to keep what I have. I must admit that I am somewhat motivated by the treat after brushing, as well as the chicken-flavored toothpaste. I like two large spoonfuls of cottage cheese mixed in with my dry food, and I eat most of that in the morning. You can give me food in the morning, and maybe a little more at night. I only eat when I feel like it. You can see from my athletic body that I'm not overweight and that overeating isn't my thing. Please keep my food dish inside, as I really dislike food that has bugs and dirt in it. I'd appreciate it if you would make sure I have water both inside and outside, as I find that drinking a lot of water keeps me looking svelt and studly.

If there's an emergency, I'd suggest you leave a message on Mom's voicemail, because I notice that she checks it all the time. Here is their schedule:

(The following paragraph contains information on the dates, times, and places Mom and Dad will be.)

Thanks for looking out for me. I think you'll discover what Mom and Dad already know: that I am a good dog and a great dog.

Yours truly,

Buddy

Writing a letter and spending some time with your dog's stand-in parents before they take over is well worth the effort. You'll put your pup, yourself, and the surrogate parents at ease. The simplest way to orient them to your dog is to have them come by while you are home and spend time together with them and your dog. Let them walk the dog while you are with them. Show them how you give medication, and then let them show you how they do it.

Taking time for training can save problems when you are too far away to make a difference. If your pet sitter isn't interested in a trial run, you might want to look elsewhere.

Traveling with Your Dog Requires Advance Planning

There are those times when you'd rather take your pup with you on a trip. That's what Betsy and Jan decided. They are two long-time friends who have traveled together for years, going on cruises, organized tours, and road trips where they stay at different hotels each night.

When Betsy got a dog, Jan was pretty sure the trips were over, especially when Betsy announced that her sweet baby, Doolittle, a rosy-colored Pomeranian, was never staying in a kennel. When she expressed her fears to Betsy, Betsy replied, "I can understand your concerns, but fear not. I did a lot of research when I decided to get a dog, and here's why I got a Pomeranian. According to my inquiries, I found they are energetic and like going for short walks, just like us. And get this. They spend long periods of time asleep or dozing. That means we can leave Doolittle in the hotel room when we go off on adventures. They don't even require much feeding, because they're more of a snack-type dog. If I leave a few chew sticks lying around, Doolittle won't damage the furniture, and once he's house-trained, he won't leave puddles anywhere. Best of all, Pomeranians, because of their size and smiling faces, are the kind of dog most people find adorable. When we take Doolittle with us, we'll meet all kinds of interesting people we might not otherwise get to know."

It all sounded convincing, so the two women started making plans for a trip. Since they had never traveled with a dog before, they decided to use the Pup Parenting Plan to help them plan ahead. Here's what they came up with.

1. The behavior that bothers me: Will we be restricted to travel in big cities when we take Doolittle with us, or are there places we can stay with the dog anywhere we go?

2. Why change is needed: We've never traveled with a dog before and we aren't sure how that will affect our trip. We like to stay in new places each night, and we aren't sure how to do that with a dog.

3. The mistake I am making: We aren't sure about Doolittle's needs when we travel, because we haven't experienced a trip with him yet. We won't know how things will be different from being at home until we go on a trip.

4. A list of possible solutions:

   - Continue our research and plan a trip using the resources available.

   - Plan a shorter trip as a trial run to help us discover what we really need to know.

   - Talk to our other friends who travel with dogs to get ideas from them.

   - Talk Betsy into changing her mind so she'll leave Doolittle at home with a house sitter.

5. Choose a solution and follow through: Betsy and Jan decided to combine the first three suggestions, and they were glad they did. They obtained AAA's newest edition of *Traveling with Your Pet*. They researched the Web, checking various hotel chains for their pet policies. They did their homework and talked to the veterinarian about what was needed for travel and called the airlines to find out what was possible. They discovered some airlines allowed dogs. A small dog could go under the seat, while a bigger dog had to stay in the baggage compartment or go as cargo (see "Air Travel" on pages 180–81).

(continued on page 182)

The United States Department of Agriculture (USDA) regulates the air transportation of pets. Their requirement is that your dog be at least eight weeks old and weaned at least five days prior to flying. It is best not to fly with an ill, very nervous, pregnant, or very old dog. The USDA also regulates the temperature levels and prohibits the shipment of animals if the temperature is below forty-five degrees or above eighty-five degrees. Check with the airline you'll be flying with, as some are even more restrictive.

Certain breeds, known as brachycephalic (snub-nosed), are very sensitive to high temperatures and will not be accepted when temperatures at any point on the planned itinerary exceed seventy-five degrees Fahrenheit (twenty-four centigrade). The following breeds are included in this restriction:

American Staffordshire terrier, Boston terrier, boxer, Brussels griffon, bull terrier, Dutch pug, English bulldog, English toy spaniel, French bulldog, Japanese spaniel (Japanese chin), Japanese pug, Pekingese, and shih tzu.

You have three options if you are planning to travel by air with your pooch:

In the cabin: This is an option only if your dog is small enough to fit in a carrier that will slide under the airplane seat in front of you with enough room for the dog to stand and turn around. Pups also have to be light enough that you can actually carry them through the airport. Some airlines, such as Southwest Airlines, don't permit dogs in the cabin at all. Other airlines have limits on the number of pets that can be in each cabin, and it is generally on a first come/first serve basis. Make your travel plans early and be sure that there is room for your pooch to accompany you. Also check with the airline on how much time you need to allow before flight time for check-in. You'll have to check-in with your pup at the counter before heading to the gate and pay the airline's fee—anywhere from thirty to a hundred dollars each way, depending upon the airline. The dog carrier also counts as one of your two-piece carry-on limit. Once on board with your pet carrier snugly under the seat, resist the urge to let your pooch out to sit in your lap. The FAA requires that the pooch remain in its closed carrier at all times while on the plane.

As checked baggage: Generally speaking, this option is available as long as the combined weight of the dog and the carrier is under one hundred pounds, and the dog must be checked in as baggage on the same flight as his pooch parents. You must make reservations for your pet in advance, as most airlines have limits on the number of animals they can take on each flight. Call your airline in advance of your travel day to confirm your reservations, your pup's reservation, and find out their rules and timing for checking your pup in. (Some airlines have a last-on/first-off policy for "checked" dogs and their humans, so as to minimize the amount of time you're separated from your dog.)

Check in at the counter well in advance of your flight, pay the airline fee for your pup, and hand Fido and crate over to airline personnel who will get the crate out to the plane for loading. You'll need a sturdy crate that is large enough for your dog to stand up, turn around, and lie down comfortably. It should have excellent ventilation, sturdy handles, and a secure latch on the door. Put something cushy on the bottom for your dog's comfort. Attach a label on the outside of the crate and use an indelible marker to write Fido's name, your name, and an address and phone number for both your home and your destination. Well before you get ready to leave for your trip, make sure your pup is comfortable in the crate by giving him plenty of opportunity to get used to it. Put it in the car and take him on a few trips around town. Never use a choke, pinch, or training collar when the dog is in the crate. Detach the leash and leave it outside the crate.

As cargo: If neither of the above two options work for you and your pup, checking your dog in as cargo is the third option. You have no guarantee of what flight your pup will be on unless you choose a "priority" or "counter-to-counter" shipping method, which is the only way to do this and be a responsible pup parent. The guidelines for crates will be the same whether you check your canine kid as baggage or as cargo.

Never give your pet sedatives or tranquilizers unless you've discussed your pup's requirements thoroughly with your veterinarian ahead of time and he's recommended one for you. These medications can interfere with your dog's ability to maintain its balance and equilibrium, which could prevent him from being able to brace himself and prevent injury. Another risk of sedatives and tranquilizers is that when accompanied with increased altitude, they can cause respiratory and cardiovascular problems.

Betsy and Jan also found out that bus trips, train trips, and cruises were out because they didn't allow dogs. Commercial carriers such as Amtrak and Greyhound have a no-pet policy, as do all cruise ships except for the *QE 2*, which has very limited options for pets. There are some charter outfits that allow dogs. A good Web site to find this sort of information is DogTravel.com. For more choices, see "Site Seeing," opposite.

Had Betsy and Jan decided to travel to another country, they would have to research which popular foreign destinations allow dogs to enter the country without a quarantine period.

Betsy and Jan decided a car trip could work well with some advance planning. Since their friends mentioned a trip they took with their pup that was really fun, the two women decided to learn all they could from their experience. Their friends told them that they loved traveling with their dog, except for the hike they had planned in a state park. When they got to the park after a very long drive, they found out that dogs weren't allowed. Because it was too hot to leave their dog in the car, they had to turn around and head back to the place they were staying without having the adventure they wanted. But later that day, they found a dog-friendly park where everyone could hike together. It had never occurred to Betsy and Jan that there were parks where dogs weren't allowed, so they were relieved to learn this information from someone else's experience.

Jan and Betsy decided to take Doolittle to the same bed-and-breakfast their friends used so they could have a two-day "dry run" before planning a bigger trip. Everything went so well that they felt confident about taking a longer trip with Doolittle.

While on their vacation, however, they learned that Doolittle liked to bark while they were gone and wasn't about to stay in the hotel room without them. This put a new spin on things, and after much research, they found a great compromise: hotels that not only allowed dogs, but also provided lists of certified pet walkers and sitters who would gladly take care of the baby for a fee. Betsy, more realistic than when she first decided her dog would go everywhere with her, was glad to use their services so that she and Jan could continue traveling together. How many of you have had encounters just like Betsy and Jan, where you found out that reality didn't always match your fantasy?

If dogs could talk, what would Doolittle say? "I always knew they'd take me with them. Who could resist a dog as cute as me? On top of that, I like it when Jan and Betsy look through their files and throw papers on the floor that they don't need. I love shredding those papers while they aren't looking."

Welcome to the World of Dog Travel

There is an entire world out there ready to welcome your pup (and you, too) with open arms. Dog lover Joan Woodard is a pro at traveling with her dogs. But even a pro can have a stressful time. Ginger, her well-traveled miniature poodle, had two frightening air travel experiences where she got to visit cities that weren't on her mom's travel schedule. Ginger managed to get to her proper destinations because of good labels on her crate and concerned airline personnel—but the many hours of delay caused Joan's hair to turn prematurely gray. (Most airlines are sympathetic to pup parents and don't mind checking to be sure that your pet carrier has been loaded on the flight before they take off. Check in with the flight attendant or captain as you board the plane and ask them to notify you.)

When Ginger died, Joan decided to get a smaller dog who could travel inside the plane with her, so she didn't have to go through the kind of trauma she did with Ginger. Her toy poodle, Teddi, weighs in at seven pounds, just the right size for the under-seat airline bag. Joan takes Teddi everywhere with her, including back and forth to her vacation home on weekends, a four-hour trip each way. Teddi sits in a special car seat designed for safety, comfort, and a good view.

When Joan celebrated her fiftieth birthday, she decided to pamper herself and her dog because Teddi is such an important part of her life. She took Teddi to Carmel, California, to stay at the Cypress Inn. Actress and animal activist Doris Day created this haven for pups and their humans to vacation together. She set everything up for doggy comfort, including a huge glass cookie jar on the front desk filled with a variety of dog biscuits ready for the taking and a sheepskin comforter for your dog at the foot of each bed. Guests are more than encouraged to have their pup with them during the cocktail hour, breakfast, or just lounging about in the common room. They also receive a list of dog-friendly restaurants in the area upon check-in. There is a special enclosed garden area specifically for doggy business with pickup bags, fire hydrant, tree stumps, and disposal bucket.

Joan said that she has to do some advance planning when she travels with her dog. Here's what she recommends. The most important thing is to make sure all vaccinations are up to date and that you have a current copy of his rabies certificate and a certificate from your veterinarian indicating that your pooch is fit for travel. If you are traveling by air, the health certificate must have been issued no more than ten days prior to your date of departure.

Even if you are traveling by car, it is a good idea to have these documents in the event you need emergency veterinary care while on the road or if you need to temporarily kennel your dog. And if you want to drop your dog off for a quick bath and blow-dry, they might require proof that your dog is up-to-date on his shots.

DOG-FRIENDLY HOTEL CHAINS

The following chains are known to be dog friendly, although policies may vary from location to location because of local health codes. Also, individual hotels within a chain might be operated by a franchise holder or owner who has different polices, so it pays to plan ahead and check in with the actual hotel you'd like to visit.

Baymont Inn & Suites	Motel 6
Clarion	Novotel
Comfort Inn & Suites	Quality Inns
Crestwood Suites Hotels	Red Roof Inn
Econolodge	Ritz Carlton
Four Seasons Hotels & Resorts	Rodeway Inn
Homestead Hotels	Sheraton
Kimpton Hotels	Sleep Inn
La Quinta Inn	Vagabond Inn
Loews Hotels	Westin
Mainstay Suites	

Some hotels and resorts, in an effort to encourage repeat business from pup parents and their pups, have developed unique programs to show how much they care. On check-in, they might provide a list of pet-friendly restaurants in the area, contacts for pet walking and pet sitting, specialized food and water bowls, complimentary bags of dog treats, a special toy, custom ID tags, and specialized bedding.

For pup parents looking for an active vacation with their pups, there are pet camps—three- to seven-day programs that include training in sports and competitive activities—for pup and parents to participate in together.

Whether traveling by air or by car, use the following checklist to be sure you remember the things that will be important for your pup's comfort and your peace of mind.

- Collar with ID and registration tags securely attached. If you are going to be at a fixed location for a while, consider having another set of ID tags made with the local address and phone number.

- Plenty of plastic bags for waste

- Bring enough food for the entire duration of your trip unless you are sure that the food your pet is used to is easily available. If you are bringing canned food, remember a can opener and spoon.

- Drinking water: Some dogs will only drink water they are accustomed to and could easily suffer from dehydration otherwise. If your dog is particular about water, bring at least two gallons of drinking water from home. After a few days in your new location, you can probably begin to mix in equal parts with the available water supply. If your pet is especially sensitive, you might need to use distilled water.

- Treats

- Food and water bowls

- A portable water bottle and/or bowl for when you are out playing

- An old bedsheet or blanket to use in the car and to cover bedding and furniture at your destination

- Toys and chew items

- Grooming items

- Flashlight for nighttime walks in unfamiliar areas

- First aid kit (details in Chapter 10)

- Medications
- Flushable baby wipes or moist towelettes for quick clean-ups
- Bedding

It Takes a Village to Raise a Dog

The more you explore, the more you'll find that the world is filled with dog people who absolutely have a love affair with their pups. Need proof? Check out Dogster.com, where pooch parents can not only show off their pooches, but connect with dog parents from all over the world. The site was started in January 2004 by a group of self-described "computer and canine geeks" in San Francisco. Six months later, the site had more than 28,000 dogs on it, each with a Web page and supportive canine parent. The site's motto is "For the love of dog."

This chapter simply wouldn't be complete without mentioning another support group for pups and their parents. The Military Pets Foster Project (NetPets.org) allows civilians to foster dogs when their moms or dads are called up for active duty. It consists of a nationwide network of individual foster homes that will house, nurture, and care for dogs and other pets for all the military and other personnel.

> If dogs could talk, we think they might say: "I love to stay at day care or travel with you. Just don't forget my blanket, my bowl, my toothbrush, my medicine, my toys, my leash, my bed, my bones I've hidden in the yard, my food, my treats, my pillow...bark, bark, bark!"

KIND AND FIRM PUP PARENTING PRINCIPLES

1. As with human children, you'll find that it takes a network of support folks to help you parent your dog. The sooner you start building your network, the easier it will be for you and your pup.

2. Research and personal recommendations are the key to finding good backup care.

3. If possible, find a person who can stay in your home to care for your dog while you are away.

4. Do dry runs with caretakers when you leave your pup at home. Take short practice/trial trips with your dog if you plan to travel with him. You'll be amazed at how much you learn with this kind of time for training.

5. Expect to find lots of dog-friendly hotels, campgrounds, restaurants, etc., when you travel, but find them before you leave home to be sure that your needs will be met on your trip.

6. Don't let a lack of advance planning ruin a trip. Leave plenty of time to find the right arrangements for your pup and schedule in advance to be sure your pup has a place to stay when you travel.

CHAPTER 10

WHEN BAD THINGS HAPPEN

"My dog is worried about the economy because Alpo is up to $3 a can. That's almost $21 in dog money."

—Joe Weinstein

Wouldn't it be nice if all you or your dog had to worry about was the price of dog food? Unfortunately, part of living with a dog is learning to deal with the struggles that come about as a result of choosing to parent a pup. If you are new at this, you should know that parenting a pup isn't all gravy. If you have a dog, you already know.

Parenting a dog exposes you to many traumas. If your dog runs away or becomes a menace to others, it can be embarrassing—and you have to do something about it. When your pups get sick, they are as helpless as little kids—caring for them can be both scary and exhausting. Dogs get injured and need to be rehabbed—it's a lot of work. Dogs get old, and they die—this is a really tough time for pup parents.

There are also possible emergencies to consider. What would happen to your dog if there was an earthquake or tornado? Have you considered who will care for your dog when you die? If you get divorced, how would you work out "custody" arrangements for your pup?

All of these very normal occurrences put a lot of stress on parents of canine kids. For some, the worst trauma happens when the dog dies. For others, it is difficult having to deal with a sick dog. In all cases, the worst cause for stress is not knowing what to expect. Reading about some of the more common traumas will give you a heads-up as to what you might anticipate as a pup parent so that you can be prepared. The more quickly you recognize reality and deal with the trauma, while still allowing yourself to have your feelings, the better you'll do. Besides the traumas over which you have no control, there are others that *you* create—but ones that you can minimize or avoid.

When a Dog Runs Away

If your dog has ever run away and didn't come back when you called, you've experienced an incident most pup parents find extremely traumatic. When your dog was found, did you breathe a sigh of relief, and then continue the very same behavior that allowed the first incident to happen, forgetting about the trauma that accompanied the event? Some pup parents have been lucky enough to get another chance to try again. Other canine parents, whose dogs have disappeared, live with the constant uncertainty as to where their pups might be. They can only wonder if s/he was hit by a car, stolen, or living with another family. They watch for their dog, hoping he or she will reappear, but after months and even years, they resign themselves to the loss.

If you have lost your dog, the first thing to do is to call the Humane Society to see if he has been picked up. Also put up flyers around the area where you last saw him. Advertise in the newspaper, offering a reward. Retrace your steps; if you were hiking and your dog wandered off, he may wander in circles looking for you in the last place he saw you. You know that all of this can be avoided if you keep your dog on a leash, but *we* know there are times that it is too tempting to let your dog run free.

A Dog Bites the Hand That Feeds Her

Just as dealing with a runaway dog can have a happy or a sad ending, so can parenting a dog who bites. And just as there is a lot of trauma when your dog runs away, a biting situation is often fraught with uncertainty. Will your dog bite again? Will your dog seriously injure someone? Worse yet, could your dog kill someone or another animal? Should your dog be put down, or can you work with the situation and ensure safety?

In the worst cases, dogs have killed or maimed humans, many of them children. Some dogs have been known to kill livestock or run in packs killing farm animals as they go. In less serious cases, dogs have snapped at, scratched, or just scared a person, but the fact that the dog behaved this way at all is definitely cause for alarm.

Tabatha was a border collie mix adopted from a shelter as a young adult. She was already displaying some extremely high levels of dog aggression, but her adoptive mom, Flo, thought she could work with it. Instead, Tabatha's behavior progressively worsened. Every time Flo walked her and Tabatha saw another dog, she went into a complete rage, lunging and barking hysterically. At those times, Flo lost all control, and all she could do was hang on to the end of the leash and wait for the rage episode to pass.

Flo's way of heading off trouble was to call to approaching dog parents, "Please don't let your dog come up to my dog. If he comes near my dog, she'll attack." In one such episode, when Flo tried to stop Tabatha from attacking another dog, she turned on Flo and bit her so severely, stitches were required. At that point, Flo decided it was time to call for help. She told Therry, "I realize I've probably waited too long and you may not be able to help me anymore because Tabatha's behavior has gotten progressively worse. It's at the point now where I haven't been able to take her out for several weeks. I really love this dog, and it upsets me that I can't take her out anymore. She needs lots of exercise, and things are becoming unbearable. You're my last hope. I'll do everything you tell me, and if it still doesn't work and I have to give up Tabatha, I'll know I've done everything I could for her."

Therry helped Flo think through the Pup Parenting Plan. Here's what they came up with.

1. The behavior that bothers me: Tabatha has become too aggressive and scary, even for me.

2. Why change is needed: Tabatha has already injured me. What's next? She could maim or kill another dog or injure someone while we walk together if I don't do something to change her behavior.

3. The mistake I am making: Therry has explained to me that I am misusing a choke collar, tugging on it and dragging Tabatha from place to place. This could be creating the problem instead of preventing it.

4. A list of possible solutions: Therry suggested the following:

   • Switch from a choke collar to a head collar.

   • Let Tabatha wear the head collar around the house to get used to it.

   • Cut down on the amount of petting I'm doing.

   • Go back to using the crate for Tabatha to sleep in and spend a little time in during the day.

   • Spend time each day with Tabatha throwing the ball for her to fetch. She's a border collie and loves retrieving things, plus, she needs the exercise outlet.

   • Bring in an expert.

5. Choose a solution and follow through: I am willing to do all of the suggestions from Therry's list, but because of the potential danger involved, I'd like Therry to work with Tabatha to help me.

When Tabatha and Therry started working together, it was an uphill battle. Tabatha didn't seem to respond to any interrupting stimulus or food treats. She'd start reacting to a dog that was as far away as a hundred yards and wouldn't stop pulling on her leash till the dog was out of sight. She couldn't be allowed in the fenced dog park to interact with other dogs because even at the fence, she became extremely defensive, raised her hackles, and flew off into her famous rage.

The only thing Therry could do was try to build her trust and confidence by bringing her around other dogs at a safe distance, and not interfere by jerking on her neck when she pulled on her leash. The head collar helped a lot, as it prevented Therry from reinforcing any behaviors that made things worse like Flo had been doing. It took Tabatha a long time to start trusting Therry to let her teach her anything. The down stay cue was the first to work. It gave her a feeling of trust and security, as Therry made sure that each time she put her on the down stay, Tabatha wasn't threatened by anybody or any other dog.

Therry continued her work with Tabatha in a park where dog parents walked by the hundreds, which meant that most of their pooches were used to other dogs and, thus, posed no threat. Every time Therry saw a dog approach from about twenty feet away, she immediately put Tabatha in the down stay because when any dog, and especially Tabatha, is moving forward, she is more likely to display aggression than when she has been given a command like the down stay, which serves to diffuse most of the problem since she's already concentrating on doing a task.

Once Tabatha got to the point that when she saw a dog approaching, she automatically went into the down stay position, it was time for Flo to learn to work with her using Therry's methods. At first she was nervous and apprehensive, but after many sessions together, she was able and willing to go out alone with her dog. The work took much longer than Flo anticipated, but eventually, Tabatha could be trusted in public and didn't have to be put down. The outcome of very serious cases of dog aggression is not often this successful. Therry attributed this success to Flo's dedication, undying faith, diligent, tireless work exposing Tabatha to other dogs, and practicing her obedience work as often as she did.

Not all pup parents who deal with a biting dog are as conscientious as Flo. Some are extremely apathetic or believe that it is okay for their dog to run free, even after their dog has proven untrustworthy. Many struggle with guilt and feel badly about any problems their dogs created, believing they should have known better or done something differently so the accident never happened in the first place. We feel that guilt is a by-product of not doing the work you know must be done. Pup parents who do their homework don't feel guilty. They feel proud of themselves and their dogs.

Responsible pup parenting is the theme of this book. If you have a dog that shows any aggressive tendencies, get the help of a behaviorist immediately and do your homework (practice) so that you and your dog are an asset to your community, instead of a liability. We know that some municipalities will give you another chance when your dog has bitten someone, but many do not. Make the best of that second chance and find out what you can change to help your dog do better.

Even Responsible Parents May Have to Euthanize their Dog

There are times, in spite of your best efforts, that you may be dealing with either a genetically flawed dog or a dog that has been trained to be aggressive and violent and can't completely reverse the early training. Spike, a brindle pit bull mix, was a case in point. At twelve weeks he barked at people other than his parents if they came near or tried to touch or pet him. Even if they offered food treats, he'd snap at them and be ready to take off their hand. His father, John, and his mom, Diana, were extensively involved in his training, which included leash manners, consistent cues, limitations of movement and freedom, and getting along with other dogs. Spike was a great student, but none of this changed how he responded to other people. Even if they were familiar faces, he still growled and snapped anytime they came near.

If you have a dog with fear and aggression tendencies like Spike, regardless of how hard you work to train your canine kid, at some point, you may have to face the realization that there are no options for your dog to live safely in a family environment. A dog like Spike will never be completely cured or fixed with any form of behavior modification. A lot of these problems could be avoided starting with the breeders, but as we've learned, there are breeders who are unconcerned about the pain and suffering you'll go through with a dog that isn't mentally or physically sound.

If your dog is like Spike, you'll need to ask yourself how attached you are to your dog and how willing and able you are to commit to a program that will help him, knowing he will never be completely mentally stable. He will never be your idea of a happy-go-lucky, friendly, trusting dog. No matter how much work you put in, you'll have to be aware that your dog could, in a stressful situation, revert back to his fear, and in doing so, could severely hurt somebody. At that point, the responsible act is to have the dog euthanized. John and Diana made this painful decision. But this didn't change the fact that they were still in love with pit bulls, so within several months, they worked with a rescue group and found another pit bull who was affectionate, enthusiastic, and a joy to live with.

Dealing with Injury and Illness

A sick dog usually gets better, and the recovery time isn't long. But there are those times when your dog's illness or injury becomes a major trauma, requiring a reshuffling of your priorities and your time.

Linda told about such an occasion when her terrier mix, BooBoo, somehow ruptured two discs in her back and had to have surgery. Linda joked that the dog "was just like her," as she had the same surgery six months earlier. (Many vets swear that the problems dogs have mirror their parents. As a pup parent, have you found this to be true?)

The vet told Linda that her dog would have to relearn how to use her hind legs. Since she couldn't use them at all when Linda brought her home from the hospital four days after her surgery, she was on puddle pads. Linda had to sling-walk her (a special leash that holds up the dog's hind legs) three times a day and keep her on a special diet. If the dog were a person, she might be in a rehab facility, but in this case, her rehab director was Linda.

"I was up very early, cleaning BooBoo up from her peeing during the night, feeding and walking her, sweating, because even though she's only forty-five pounds, deadweight is deadweight. Then I had to feed the other dog, Bear, who was freaked out. Then I'd go to work, come home at lunch to repeat the cleanup, then back to work, then home. A friend would come to help me in the evening so I could bathe Boo's back end, because urine on dog fur and skin is not a good thing.

"By the second day she was home, she wagged her tail, and by the fourth day she was putting some weight on her back legs. Her recovery was incredible. She used the sling for about two or three weeks, and by mid-July was able to walk without it. Imagine trying to poop with someone holding your butt and hoping she doesn't drop you."

Would you be willing and able to do what Linda did to help with her dog's recovery? And would you keep your sense of humor while doing it?

For various reasons, some dogs end up having a leg amputated, or they lose the ability to put weight on one of their legs. Rather than trying to lift a sixty- to ninety-pound dog into your car, you can purchase a telescoping pet ramp (about $150) to save your back. The Paw Step Ramp allows your dog to climb into an SUV and onto her bed. Orvis also sells a car step and a bumper adapter for older, stiff-legged dogs, or you could check out BottomsUpLeash. com for a hind-leg halter for dogs with arthritis and hip dysplasia. (If you haven't discovered this already, the Web is a great place to find resources for your pup!)

Dealing with a Disaster Requiring Evacuation

You probably know what to do if your dog gets sick, but have you ever considered what could happen in a natural disaster? No matter how remote the chance of experiencing one, you might want to do a little advance planning—not only for yourself, but also for your dog. What if you had to evacuate an area? What would you do with your dog? What if a tornado or fire or earthquake or flood threatened your home? Minimally, we suggest that you stock up on food, water, and First aid supplies and have a pet carrier handy. You might also want to have an evacuation plan, preferably one that includes your pup. In times of disaster, with so much chaos going on, it would be easy to think someone else has taken care of the dog.

Annie McGuire of Lake Effect Dog Training in Grand Rapids, Michigan, has kindly offered details about what you might want to put into your dog's First aid kit. We provide it here for your help. It is one of the most complete and helpful aids we found to assist you in being prepared for medical problems. We have consulted veterinarian Barbara Farrell, DVM, to confirm the dosages. Some of you may be satisfied with a more simple First aid kit or a specialized kit that can be obtained at most pet stores.

WHAT TO PUT IN YOUR DOG'S FIRST AID KIT

Assembling a canine First aid kit for home or travel use is fairly simple. In fact, it's pretty easy to assemble a kit that will serve both human and canine members of your family!

Before reading further, know that I am *not* a veterinarian. The contents of my First aid kit were assembled using common sense and my experiences with my own dogs. [For this reason, we contacted Dr. Barbara Farrell, DVM, to make sure that the information and dosages were accurate. Thank you, Dr. Farrell.]

The first thing you need for a good First aid kit is a suitable container. We use a fishing tackle-type box. On the outside, with permanent marker, label the box **FIRST AID** on all sides—in an emergency, someone else might have to locate and use this kit. Tape to the inside of the box lid a card with the following information:

- Your name, address, and phone number

- The name and phone number of someone to contact in an emergency who will take care of your dogs if you are incapacitated

- Your dogs' names and any information about any medications they take, any allergies, or significant medical conditions
- The name and phone number of your vet
- A list of common medications, their general dosages, and the specific dose for the weights of your own dogs: For example:

  Benadryl: 1mg per pound, every 8 hours

  Hydrogen peroxide to induce vomiting: 1–3 tsp every 10 minutes until dog vomits

  Pepto-Bismol: 1 tsp per 5 pounds per 6 hours

  Kaopectate: 1 ml per pound per 2 hours

Never ever give acetaminophen (Tylenol, which is toxic to the liver) or ibuprofen (Nuprin, Motrin, Advil, etc.). Ibuprofen is very toxic and fatal to dogs at low doses. Only aspirin is safe for dogs, and buffered aspirin or ascriptin is preferred to minimize stomach upset. [Dr. Farrell recommends that you consult with your veterinarian or an emergency clinic before giving any medication. They are a phone call away and will help you make sure the dosage meets the requirements for your dog based on breed, age, and health history. But do have these medications on hand in a First aid kit.]

Give liquid meds using an oral syringe tucked into the side of the dog's mouth, holding jaws closed (rather than straight down the throat and risking getting liquid into the lungs).

Its also a good idea to keep copies of your dog's vaccination records, including a copy of the rabies certificate, in the First aid kit or in a packet in your car. I keep packets with shot records, what heartworm preventative the dogs get and which day of the month it should be given, emergency contact information, and my vet's name and phone number in *each* car and in my dog show equipment bag. In addition, the emergency contact and vet information are clearly posted on my refrigerator door at home where anyone who needs it can find it easily. You never know when you may be incapacitated in an accident and your dogs may be in the hands of a complete stranger who will need this information.

Things to Put in the First Aid Kit

- Elastic bandage
- Cotton gauze bandage wrap: 1.5-inch width and 3-inch width

- Vet wrap: 2-inch width and 4-inch width (4 inch is sold for horses)
- First aid tape
- Cotton gauze pads
- Regular adhesive bandages
- Cotton swabs
- Benadryl (Check with your vet to confirm dosages before using.)
- Pepto-Bismol tablets
- Liquid bandages (useful for patching abrasions on pads)
- Iodine tablets (if you hike and camp in areas where the stream water may not be safe for consumption without first treating with iodine or boiling)
- Oral syringes (for administering liquid oral medicines, getting ear drying solution into ears, etc...very useful!)
- Needle and thread
- Safety pins in several sizes
- Razor blade (paper-wrapped for protection)
- Matches
- Tweezers
- Hemostat (useful for pulling ticks, thorns, large splinters, etc.)
- Small blunt-end scissors
- Canine rectal thermometer (one made specifically for dogs)
- Antibiotic ointment (such as Bacitracin, Betadine, or others)
- Eye-rinsing solution (simple mild eye wash)
- Small bottle of 3% hydrogen peroxide
- Small bottle of isopropyl (rubbing) alcohol
- Alcohol or antiseptic wipes (in small individual packets)
- Small jar of petroleum jelly
- Specific medications your dog may need (for allergies, seizures, etc.)

Loving Your Dog Enough to Give Her Up

It's likely that you have heard the story of King Solomon and the two mothers who both claimed the same baby. Wise King Solomon offered to cut the baby in half so both of the mothers could share the baby equally. Of course, the "real" mother spoke up quickly and denied that she was the real mother so she could save the baby's life. Likewise, sometimes the most loving thing you can do is give your dog away.

The Nelsens had a wonderful and affectionate golden retriever named Britt. When the last of their children left home, they also lost their live-in nanny, who was Britt's primary caretaker. Barry, Jane's husband, was assigned to an out-of-town project that allowed him to come home only on weekends, while Jane was engaged in an extensive travel program for lectures and workshops. Britt was left alone way too much and was becoming lethargic. Jane and Barry knew they could no longer provide the kind of love Britt needed.

Fortunately, they were able to find a fabulous place for Britt—a nursing home where the director understood the health benefits that animals can bring to people. They moved Britt into the home, where she became an "honorary resident." Britt was a very affectionate dog who was able to give and receive so much love. She would wander from room to room where the senior citizens were delighted to see her. They would talk to Britt and pet her—and Britt was in heaven. During quiet times, Britt slept under a desk at the feet of the director. Britt was able to enjoy a quality of life in her "old age" that would not have been possible had she remained with the Nelsens. They loved her enough to give her up.

If Something Happens to You

Have you made arrangements for your pup if something should happen to you? If you haven't put something in writing, your dog may end up not cared for or euthanized. A 1993 change in the Uniform Probate Code, a legal model used by many state systems, allows trusts for pets that continue for the pet's lifetime. The states quickly followed with laws of their own. Now, by adding only a sentence or two to an ordinary will, pet owners can designate an amount to be spent on the pet and a trustee to carry that out under court supervision.

If you would like to set up a legal document that describes the continued care and maintenance of a particular animal, refer to *When Your Pet Outlives You* by David Congalton and Charlotte Alexander. It spells out the steps to setting up such a trust. Briefly, the steps are the following: select a trustee, select a caretaker, bequest your pet to the trustee, avoid excessively funding the trust, request a desired standard of living for your pet, place time limits on the trust, use the trustee as a watchdog, provide complete identification, name a remainder beneficiary, and provide instructions for handling your pet's death.

For more information about setting up a trust for your dog, check with LexisNexis at Lawyers.com. There may be less complex ways to set up a caretaking situation, but you do need to think about your canine kids and how they will be taken care of if you aren't around to do the job. Make sure you include information about the care of your dog with your will or trust information, including the kind of information we covered in the letters to caregivers found in Chapter 9. If you're looking to avoid the legal "hassles," your dog may not end up enjoying the kind of life she had with you.

Dogs and Divorce

Death isn't the only time that you may need a legal document, or at the least, an agreement with another person for the care of your dog. Divorce is another traumatic event that many families deal with. It's widespread knowledge that parents worry about how divorce will affect their children's lives, and many couples stay together for the sake of the kids. But consider this: Some couples also stay together for the sake of their dogs, worrying how divorce will affect their canine kids. When a divorce becomes inevitable, there are hard decisions to make about who will care for the dogs. Once the divorce happens, changes have to be made involving the care of the dogs, visitation, and dealing with dogs who may now live in two different families.

Every situation is unique, but Beth's story encompasses many of the issues that other families struggle with. Beth and Gavin were pup parents to two pugs, Rosie and Willoughby, and a German shepherd named Ruby. Beth knew that Gavin couldn't live without the pugs. He carried Rosie around in a baby pouch, and when Willoughby joined the family, he slept curled up with Rosie. But Beth wasn't sure that she could stand being without the pugs, either. She said that one of the reasons she didn't leave sooner was that she couldn't figure out how to "divide" the dogs. Like many parents do, she handled the confusion by not making a decision. Finally, she knew she had to rise above the situation and let Gavin take Rosie and Willoughby, while Ruby remained with her.

Beth shared that the dogs have handled the divorce well. You can help your dogs deal with trauma by creating new routines with them. That's how Beth helped her dog make the transition. She talked to Ruby a lot about what was going on. (We've said that when training your pup, use as few words as possible. But when you are comforting your dog, a soothing conversation does wonders.) She also started "Ruby Night" on Wednesdays so the two of them could have some special time together. Beth comes home early and the two of them go to the cemetery. They call it the "Dead People's Park." Since it's fenced in and Beth doesn't have to worry about Ruby escaping, Beth takes Ruby off her leash to run around. When they come home, Ruby goes out in the garage and lays on her bed with a big chew bone while Beth rides her stationary bike.

When a couple splits up, they go through a lot of the trauma that Beth did over what to do with the dogs. Some folks end up giving their dogs to a rescue organization. Others end up paying "dog support" to the parent who keeps the dog. Some people even share custody of Fido.

Regardless of the decision about dog custody, the best way to ease the dog(s) through a breakup is to disrupt what they are used to as little as possible. If they are used to being around children, keep them with the kids. If they have one parent who they spend the most time with, let the dog stay with that parent. If the dog is used to living with another dog, keep the dogs together if at all possible. If your dogs are used to being fed as soon as you get out of bed, keep feeding them at that time. If your noncustodial mate was the one who walked them after dinner, it's up to you to carry on that routine.

Remember that your dogs have been picking up all the tension in the home, just like children do, and they may act out for a while. But *don't punish*. Be kind and firm and continue with positive pup parenting. And don't expect your dog to fall in love with new family members, if you go down that path. Give the dog time to get used to new people if you change your living situation and add other humans to the home.

When a Brother or Sister Dog Dies

When Pancho, an adorable Chihuahua, lost his older brother, Taco, everyone in the family was worried how Pancho would handle the loss. Soon, it was obvious that Pancho was doing much better than the rest of the family, who was devastated by Taco's death. Pancho seemed to thrive on being the center of attention and having all the special time with his family members.

But not all dogs handle the death of another dog as easily as Pancho did. Some grieve extensively. In one family, when the first dog died, the second dog, never a snuggler, insisted on sleeping in bed with Mom and Dad for six months, cuddled in between the two of them. And when they got another dog, he refused to let them pet the new baby for several months while he took his time adjusting to the "interloper."

Often dogs will act out their grief. Chelsea, a West Highland terrier who lost her poodle sister, went on a rampage. When the family came home, it looked like the house had been burglarized. Chelsea, normally an even-tempered dog, had taken pillows and stuffed animals off the beds and pulled toys out of the doll house and chewed on them. The family members realized that in their grief, no one had thought to comfort her.

How *do* you comfort your dog? Allow her to grieve in whatever way she uses. Your dog has experienced a loss. Most dogs will begin to recover within a day or two. Then you can begin new routines, make your dog feel special, spend time with your dog, and trust that she can move on. You do not have to run out and get another dog to replace the one who died. With time, your dog can adjust to being an only dog.

Your Aging Dog—Early Hints of the End

Dogs are living to be older and older, probably as a result of their excellent care and the advances in veterinary medicine. What this means is that pup parents are now dealing with geriatric dogs and the host of issues that accompany old age. According to Dr. Johnny Hoskins, a veterinarian from Baton Rouge, Louisiana, (as reported in the *New York Times*), "People are not looking for excuses to do away with [their dogs] the way they used to. They want them to live as long as there's quality of life."

The last few years of your dog's life can be very expensive and challenging for both of you. As Dr. Hoskins said, years ago, you might have chosen to put your dog down. Now you have many other choices. As a preventive measure, you can ask your veterinarian to do a senior wellness exam once or twice a year to help spot problems before they get out of hand. Once issues emerge, you still have many other alternatives to euthanasia for dealing with the problems that come from aging.

Did you ever think you'd be using doggy diapers, elevated feeding bowls, orthopedic beds, hind leg halters, ramps, surgeries, medications, and massages? All of these and more are available to help your dog through his geriatric years. In fact, some folks have been known to take better care of their dogs than they do their relatives. Perhaps the question you must ask yourself is whether you are doing all the special treatments for your dog or for yourself. Whatever the answer, these last years can be very traumatic.

It's not just the physical issues you have to adjust to. The emotional roller coaster you go on during your dog's last years can be very trying. First, you feel helpless as you watch your dog suffer physically when there is little you can do to help. You see the deterioration, you know it's irreversible, and yet, your dog still wags his tail when you put his food out and gets excited when you take his leash off the hook to go for a walk. You watch your dog have good days and bad days. Sometimes, you think it's the end, and then your dog will act like he did when he was a pup, maybe for a week at a time. You tell yourself you must have been catastrophizing, thinking your dog was getting ready to die. You spend as much time on the phone with your vet as you do with your best friend, calling to ask if you should bring your dog in. "No," the vet reassures you, "he was in two weeks ago and he looked great. He's just getting old."

Then your dog starts doing things he never did before. He stands at the door to go outside. You put him outside, and he turns around and stands at the door, barking, to come inside. He comes inside and he stands at the wall near the door, barking, to go back out. Your heart breaks. Is he blind? Is he having a "senior moment"? Is this early Alzheimer's? He has accidents in the house or defecates while he is laying down because he can't get up or posture anymore to have his bowel movements. You clean him up and clean the rug and the floor, all the time having mixed feelings. You know he can't help it, and yet, you resent the extra work—or you are already mourning his passing, even though his actual passing may be months or even years away. Living with the unknown plays havoc with your emotions.

Before advances in medicine, your dog may have died in his sleep, or been so ill that the only alternative was euthanasia. Before stricter leash laws and changes in attitudes about parenting your dog, she may have met her end in front of a car. Now, it's sometimes up to you to decide when he should go. You know that the moment you get out of denial and realize your dog is aging, and it's irreversible.

Lynn's denial system caved one day when she was walking her dogs. They were in a place they always walked without leashes. Lynn, distracted as she talked to a friend, suddenly realized the dogs weren't running ahead like usual. She turned around and there they were, lagging far behind.

She saw Buddy struggling with his legs. His arthritis seemed to be worse than ever, and he looked like he was in a lot of pain. Magic wasn't doing much better. She dragged along near Buddy, but that was understandable, as she had recently had a surgery to remove a cancerous tumor from her rear leg. Lynn's heart sank when she saw them, realizing just how old they were getting and how little time she probably had left with them.

Her friend must have had the same thought because she asked, "When Buddy and Magic aren't around anymore, will you and Hal be getting another dog?" Lynn explained that she couldn't think about something like that while her dogs were still with her, but the question was another reality blow, bringing to her attention something she hadn't wanted to look at. Her dogs were old and would probably die soon. She vowed in that moment to enjoy the time she had left with them as much as possible. And she secretly wished that when her dogs died, it would be in their sleep without a lot of suffering. What pup parent wouldn't want that?

As it turned out, Buddy deteriorated so badly and was in so much pain that Lynn and Hal decided to have him euthanized. Lynn couldn't bear to watch him die, so she said good-bye before Hal took him to the vet. Hal sobbed and sobbed as he held Buddy while he died.

Losing a Dog to Cancer

Cancer is the number one cause of death among dogs in the U.S., according to an article in *HealthyPet*. But, the article went on to say, cancer "is the most curable of all chronic diseases in pets…" It's good to know that a word that used to strike fear in the hearts of a dog parent doesn't necessarily mean that the dog has been given a death sentence. Many pup parents are walking around with dogs who have recovered from cancer. While this may be true, there are still many dogs who die from the disease, and losing a dog to cancer can be as hard on the pup parent as losing a human to cancer.

When Therry lost her German shepherd, Smoke Von Patrick, fondly called My Son, to cancer at age ten, she lost more than a dog. He was her working partner, helping her train other dogs. He taught the dogs respect. He played endlessly with them. His patience never ran out, and he never overdisciplined any dog. He got along with every dog because he didn't evoke aggressive feelings in them. Puppies worshiped him and turned themselves inside out, wriggling, and flipping themselves over to please him.

When My Son developed a large cancerous tumor on his spleen at age ten , even surgery to remove his spleen wasn't enough to save his life. The cancer had already metastasized.

There are families who have spent more than $10,000 on chemo and radiation therapy for their dogs, often taking on second jobs or sacrificing their own plans for the sake of the dog. Therry decided against chemo because it had never proven successful for this type of cancer.

The news of his condition was the saddest news Therry had ever heard. For her, losing My Son was doubly sad. On the one hand, he was like a family member. On the other hand, losing him was losing a teammate. Therry had to find a whole new way of doing her work. She was convinced she couldn't provide as much to her clients without his help, and her work was never the same for her once he died.

Just as Therry knew when it was the end, so do most pup parents who have dogs that deteriorate with age. They all say that there are clues from the dog. When your dog isn't enjoying her life anymore, that's a message that it might be time for extreme measures. If your dog stops eating or doesn't get excited about going for a walk, or can barely stand, or gets a glassy look in her eyes, it may be time to make that call to the veterinarian, as hard as it may be.

Most canine parents let their dog make the decision for them, and most dogs do. Freelance writer Eileen Mitchell wrote the following in the *San Francisco Chronicle* about Kim Felch and her little dog, Kacey, who lost her sight: "For hours she was sitting in one spot with her head hung low. She seemed depressed.... I kneeled and looked at her beautiful little face tucked in my hands. Even though she had no eyes it was like she was looking right back at me, saying, 'I'm ready, it's time.'"

A Dog's Death Is Inspiration for Others

Chloe was an Akita who came into her grandmother's life just as she got her first taste of retirement. Chloe was going to live with Grandma for a few weeks, but because of circumstances, she stayed long enough to give everyone an experience of unconditional love. When Chloe died of cancer, her pooch grandma put together a memorial to her that she passed out to the neighbors who had come to enjoy Chloe's visits. It contained a picture of the beautiful dog along with stories of her times with her grandparents. It also contained the story of her death, which we're sharing here.

"In late June, we went to the vet's with a limp, which I thought some arthritis medication would take care of. Tests, x-rays, and biopsy surgery concluded Chloe had osteosarcoma, or bone cancer. The next step would be a front left limb amputation near the shoulder with six months of chemo treatments to follow, with no guarantee that the cancer cells wouldn't spread when disturbed. We reached out to the Internet to dog owners who were in our situation and read of their solutions. Based on what we read, we decided instead on pain pills until a morphine patch was needed in the end.

"Our family gathered on October 10th to celebrate Chloe making it to her eleventh birthday. She was a sick cancer patient impersonating a happy birthday girl, enjoying pizza, spareribs, ice cream, and cake. Chloe actually seemed to smile at times.

"The final day was peaceful. Chloe laid on the cool grass in front of the house watching people walking by…she got up to greet the vet and wagged her tail as he bent down to pet her on the head. At sunset, among some of the people who loved her, euthanasia took but a few minutes and it was over. Chloe, free from pain, is resting in the 'Gentle Giant Area' in the lovely Napa Pet Cemetery alongside a twelve-year-old neighbor, a St. Bernard named Kong."

The memorial paper ended with the following poem called "If It Should Be," that may be inspirational to you when you experience the death of your dog. The author is unknown, but we're sure that if dogs could talk, it is exactly what they would say.

If Dogs Could Talk:

If it should be that I grow weak and pain should keep me from my sleep,

Then you must do what must be done, for this last battle cannot be won.

You will be sad, I understand. Don't let your grief then stay your hand.

For this day more than all the rest, your love for me must stand the test.

We've had so many happy years. What is to come can hold no fears.

You'd not want me to suffer so. The time has come. Please let me go.

Take me where my needs they'll tend. And please stay with me until the end.

Hold me firm and speak to me, until my eyes no longer see.

I know in time that you will see the kindness that you did for me.

Although my tail its last has waved, from pain and suffering I've been saved.

Please do not grieve—it must be you who had this painful thing to do.

We've been so close, we two, these years. Don't let your heart hold back its tears.

We know this chapter is full of sadness, but we are sure you also feel the love. Would any of these parents give up their experiences as pup parents if they knew how traumatic it could be at times? We're sure the answer is no. When all is said and done, these parents know what you know. The love and joy your dog brings into you life makes it all worth it.

KIND AND FIRM PUP PARENTING PRINCIPLES

1. When the hard times come, work at being realistic and allow yourself to have your feelings. This will help you and your pup move forward to deal with what is needed.

2. Overindulgence is a surefire way to create anxiety problems and other dysfunctional relationship issues with your dog.

3. Most, if not all, runaway situations can be avoided by keeping your dog on a leash or in a confined area.

4. Take biting very seriously and get help quickly to avoid worse problems.

5. First aid and other emergency plans usually mirror what you would do for humans. Don't leave your dog uncared for in case of an emergency.

6. Enjoy your dog's elder years, but don't be afraid to make the hard decision when it's time to let your dog go.

CONCLUSION

THE FIFTH *L*: IT'S ALL ABOUT LOVE

"If the history of all the dogs who have loved and been loved by the race of man could be written, each history of a dog would resemble all the other histories. It would be a love story."

—James Douglas, *from* Dog Days *by Hulton Getty*

Pup parents know there are very few relationships in life as rewarding and wonderful as the one between them and their dog. It's a kind of love affair that goes both ways. Your dog loves you unconditionally and shows you that love daily. You love your dog and want the best for your canine kid.

Many of you fill your deepest need for belonging by living with a dog. This might even be the main reason why so many of you chose to be pup parents. As one dog mom said about her kid, "We are a couple. I like someone to sleep with (she sleeps at the foot of my bed), someone to talk to (she listens to every word I say without judgments or advice), someone who is excited when I get home (she greets me every day as if I've been gone for a week), and someone to cuddle with when I watch TV (she likes all the same shows I do and never fights for the remote)."

This doesn't mean that there aren't times when you question why you became a dog parent in the first place or whether you will parent another dog after yours dies. Some of you will entertain the notion from time to time of having the freedom that comes if you choose not to have another dog. You can come and go as you please and avoid all those messy times when your pup tore your place apart, ruined your carpets, or shed on all your clothes.

But most dog people feel lonely without a dog. The house seems empty and something isn't quite right. There is a hollow sound in the air. Dog people forget the hard times, just like human mothers forget the pain of labor and childbirth. You look through your photo album and see the picture of your dog dressed in a cute reindeer hat—and you've forgotten what you went through to get that picture. You've erased from your memory the choking sounds your pup made every time you put on the reindeer ears or the number of times the camera hit the ground when Fido knocked over the tripod with his wagging tail. So what if his eyes are closed in the picture and you can still hear the expletive coming from your mouth just as the shutter clicked? It's all worth it. Each time you look at the Christmas card, you smile and think how lucky you are to be a pup parent.

It is plain and simple: when you're a dog person, you love dogs— and you appreciate the great capacity of dogs to demonstrate love for humans. Stories like those that follow don't surprise you in the least, but upon hearing them you probably get a bit misty-eyed.

- During 9/11, one dog was believed to have saved 967 lives, suffered smoke inhalation, severe burns on all four paws, and a broken leg. Mayor Rudy Giuliani awarded her the Canine Medal of Honor of New York, the first canine to win such an honor.

- A rottweiler howled every time his colicky human baby brother cried. The two wouldn't stop howling and crying until Mom sat down and comforted both of them with the sound of her hair dryer.

- A little Cavalier King Charles spaniel comforted his mom when she found out she had a lump in her breast and thought she had cancer. While his mom cried on the couch, he jumped up next to her, leaned against her, put his paws around her neck and stayed until her husband came home.

- Lynn's schnauzer, Magic, has an uncanny knack for knowing who needs some special cuddling. She loves to attend Lynn's group therapy retreats, where she lays on the rug under the coffee table, until the first sound of sniffles. Then she's up and into the lap of the crying person. Sometimes, people don't even have to show an outward sign of sadness or hurt before Magic has intuited their need to feel the warmth and love of a dog. Group members marvel at her perceptiveness and appreciate her comfort.

There are dogs trained as therapy dogs who make regular visits to nursing homes, hospitals, and schools. Their volunteer pup parents take them to cheer folks up as well as provide comfort, companionship, and something special to look forward to. There are countless examples of otherwise nonresponsive patients suddenly able to move an arm to pet a dog or smile at the sensation of a dog's kiss on their hand.

Dogs can show love by guarding you or your home. Lynn's Samoyed, Buddy, showed his love by guarding the perimeter of their vacation home that borders on a national forest. One day, a large black bear was heading toward the house. There had been incidents of bears actually getting into people's homes and leaving a trail of chaos and destruction behind, so when Lynn saw the bear lumbering up to the deck, she decided to give Buddy a chance to earn his keep. She called for him and he came running to her side. "Buddy," she said, "go explain to that bear that this is our house and he isn't welcome inside." Buddy took off at a run to confront the bear who turned and ran to the nearest tree, climbing it faster than one would believe possible. Once the bear was up the tree, Buddy backed away and sat at a safe distance until the bear climbed out of the tree and departed into the woods. A job well done!

We've noticed that a lot of literature contains stories about the love for a dog. The following excerpt from Robert Parker's *Back Story* is one of our favorites:

"Pearl was tearing around in Susan's backyard with an azalea bush she had uprooted. Hawk and Susan and I were having an entirely delicious sangria, which I had made, and eating cheese with French bread and cherries.

"'What am I going to do,' Susan said. 'She uproots my shrubs, eats my flowers, digs huge holes.'

"'I could shoot her,' Hawk said.

"'Shush,' Susan said. 'She'll hear you.'"

Parker's stories about Pearl make us laugh because it is clear that Pearl is more than a dog. She is Susan's "baby," like a lot of our dogs are to us. There are times when reading Parker that you'll think Pearl could use a bit more kind and firm parenting (whose dog couldn't?), but mostly, the loving relationship is mutually respectful.

This love affair with our pets has fueled one of the country's healthiest industries with sales of pet products now around $31 billion, outpacing the popular human toy industry and the candy industry. Pup parents have choices available today that have never before been an option.

We're not worried about the dog dressed in designer clothes. If your pocketbook and interest runs in that direction, have fun. There is no end to what you can buy your dog. Just remember that those toys, designer clothes, fancy bedding and furniture, and bakery treats that rival those of humans are no substitute for a walk or playtime or training practice. The INsecurity blanket you can rub on your skin and leave for your dog doesn't make up for quality time, and the Talk to Me Treat Ball, where you can record a message that will play back when your pup hits the ball around, isn't a substitute for your presence.

If you can afford it, you can treat your dogs like royalty, indulging them in massages and gourmet dinners from pet menus at some of the country's finest hotels. You can leave your dogs at the America Dog and Cat Hotel luxury rooms in Las Vegas. The 75,000-square-foot facility near McCarran International Airport features private suites, color TVs, manicures, and limo transfers. But when all is said and done, don't forget to throw a ball for your dog to fetch, scratch him behind the ears, and rub his belly.

Some pup parents attend Doggie Happy Hour where about 75 dogs join each other Tuesday and Thursday afternoons from April through October in the courtyard of the Old Town Holiday Inn Select in Alexandria, Virginia. The pups get dog bones and water while their parents mingle with others, drink cocktails, and share their passion for pets. Since both pups and their parents are having a good time, it's a great way to have fun with your dog. Maybe there's a similar "yappy hour" near you.

You could also take your dog to the San Francisco Pet Pride Day. Here they can get a massage, march in the parade dressed in costume, try their luck on an agility course, or rock to the sounds of James Brown's "I Feel Good." Or you could attend the San Francisco Bark and Whine Ball, where dogs and their parents dress to kill, often in matching outfits.

So far, we haven't heard a single dog asking for these things. (Of course, food is another matter. Dogs constantly beg for food…) Yet canine kid parents are buying so many items for their pets, treating them better than some humans, and taking them everywhere.

So, is it possible to love a dog too much?

Yes, when we let our love of our pooch cloud our otherwise appropriate behavior, as evidenced by the woman who thought it was adorable to have her two little Yorkies in her lap while she drove. It stopped being adorable when they crawled out of her lap and started climbing in her hair. After several near misses, she decided it wasn't worth having a car accident to meet her dogs' wants (not needs).

Too much love can also be dangerous to your dog. We've all seen overweight dogs, and we shake our heads at how any owner could let his dog get so chubby. Teeny von Weenie, a dachshund, grew a belly bigger than her daddy's because whenever he had a snack, Teeny looked at him with baleful eyes until he relented and gave her one, too. He said, "No dog would look that unhappy unless she really *needed* a treat. I love my dog and I'm not going to deny her anything." Right? Wrong! Your job is to love your dog enough to practice kind and firm pup parenting on a daily basis.

It takes time for the ideas in this book to become second nature. Some changes will come quicker than others. Some of you may say, "If I could do this with my dog with so little effort, maybe I could do this with my kids." Others will think, "I can do this with my kids, but it's really hard for me to be kind and firm with my dog." Don't give up on yourself—or your dog. Soon you'll be writing a love story of your own.

If dogs could talk, we think they'd say: "I love you, Mom and Dad."

ABOUT THE AUTHORS

Lynn Lott, Jane Nelsen, and Therry Jay are all believers in helping adults make small changes that will create big results in the family. They share the same basic philosophy of mutual respect and agree that it is the adult's job to help family members learn and grow in a safe and nonpunitive setting. Together, the authors are a great and powerful team.

Lynn holds two Masters degrees in counseling and psychology and is lovingly called the "female Dr. Phil" by her clients and friends. A well-known and busy family therapist, Lynn has taught parenting; trained family therapists; served as an associate professor at Sonoma State University in California; traveled the United States and Canada to present workshops for parents, teachers, and therapists; and founded and directed The Family Education Centers of Sonoma County. She is a Diplomate in her professional organization, the North American Society of Adlerian Psychology (NASAP), the highest honor of achievement.

Lynn's self-help books include three in the "Positive Discipline" series, *Do-It-Yourself Therapy*, *Chores without Wars*, and *Seven Steps on the Writer's Path* with novelist Nancy Pickard. She is also the coauthor of *Madame Dora's Fortune-Telling*

Cards. Lynn is as comfortable on a radio or TV talk show as she is skiing down the black diamond runs in the winter. She is the mother of two and stepmother of two, living with her husband, Hal, and canine kid, Magic, in California and Florida.

Jane earned her doctorate degree in educational psychology from the University of San Francisco. She is a prolific writer with eighteen books in print, and more on the way. Her best known books include *Positive Discipline: Raising Self-Reliant Children in a Self-Indulgent World, Positive Discipline A–Z, Positive Discipline: The First Three Years, Positive Discipline for Preschoolers,* and *Positive Discipline for Teenagers.* Her books have sold almost two million copies and have been translated into more than a dozen languages. Jane is an internationally known speaker who travels the globe to present keynotes and workshops in the United States, Japan, Columbia, Germany, Holland, Singapore, Belgium, and Australia. She has been a guest on numerous television talk shows and radio shows and has been interviewed and quoted extensively in newspapers and magazines. She founded Empowering People Books, Tapes and Videos (the Positive Discipline Web site) and Positive Discipline Associates' training program. Jane is also a Diplomate in Adlerian Psychology.

The mother of seven children and grandmother to eighteen grandchildren, when she's not on a plane going to deliver a lecture, Jane resides with her husband, Barry, in Salt Lake City and San Clemente, California. She is a dog lover and former dog parent who now travels too extensively to have a respectful relationship with a dog.

Therry Jay has been working professionally with animals and the people who own them since 1971, starting as an in-home animal behaviorist, then moving on to founding and instructing at the Chaparral K-9 School and Intern Program for Trainers/Behavior

Consultants in California. She has worked as a breeder, showed dogs, did police K-9 training, and boarded and trained dogs. She currently works full-time training horses. Therry is known for her passionate, intense, and thought-provoking work. For years, her greatest mission in life was to inform and educate dog owners to understand and communicate with their pets.

Therry is a member of the Association for Pet Dog Trainers, a professional organization of individual trainer/behavior consultants with members throughout the United States and the world, dedicated to educating and training pet dogs and owners. She is also involved in rescuing and re-homing abandoned, unwanted, and homeless pets and works closely with local rescue groups. She was affiliated with the Cotati Small Animal Hospital for years, where she oversaw the fifteen-kennel boarding facility.

INDEX

Underscored page references indicate boxed text and tables.

C

Camps, pet, <u>185</u>
Cancer, death from, 206–7
Canine classification models, 148–49
Caretakers. *See also* Pet sitters/pet walkers
  avoiding inconsistencies from, 169–73
  after death of pup parent, 58, 201
  trial runs with, 173, 177
  variety of, 166
  written instructions or letter for, 173–77
Car safety, 87–89
Celebrity dogs, <u>60</u>
Chaining, problems with, 84–85
Chasing games, 24–27
Chewing, 30–32
Children, involved in dog care, 27–29
Choice of dog
  life phase influencing, 51–58
  lifestyle influencing, 38–41, 108–9
Classifieds, caution about finding dog from, 66
Cleanup after dogs, 78–79
Clicker training, for teaching walking, 126
Collars, training, 121–22, 192, 193
Comfort (turtle) personality, 150, 151–52, <u>156–57</u>, <u>158</u>, 163, 164
Communication skills of dogs, 114–16
Confinement. *See also* Crates; Ex-pens; Fencing options; Tie-downs; Trolley system
  for puppies, 95–96, 106–8
Control (eagle) personality, 150, 153–54, <u>156–57</u>, <u>160</u>, 163, 164
Couch sleeping, discouraging, 47–49
Crates, 34, 50, 90, 95, 106–7, 108, 112
Crying, 98, 109–10, 136
Cues, for obedience training, 116–17, 119, 127–28, 129

Curb link choke collar, 121–22
Custody after divorce, 202–3

D

Daily care needs, influencing choice of dog, 39–40
Day care, 80, 91, 172, 173
Death
  of dogs
    from aging, 204–6
    brother or sister dog, 203–4
    from cancer, 206–7
    inspiration from, 208, <u>209</u>
  of pup parent, planning for pet care after, 58, 200–201
Defecation in house. *See* Housebreaking accidents; Potty training
Destructiveness, of puppies, 98–99, 105–10. *See also* Home-alone problems
Disasters requiring evacuation, 196–99
Dishes, dog, 96
Disrespect
  as pup parenting mistake, 19–20
  story about changing, 27–29
Dog groups, characteristics of, <u>76–77</u>
Doghouse, 85
Dog sitters or walkers. *See* Pet sitters/pet walkers
Drag lead, 134, 135

E

Emotional needs of dogs, 19
Empty nesters, dog selection considerations for, 56–57
Euthanasia
  for aggressive dogs, 194–95
  for aging dog, 204, 205, 206
Evacuation, disasters requiring, 196–99
Ex-pens, 50–51, 96, 112
Expenses
  benefits of ownership outweighing, 62–63